Let the Earth Rejoice

How a Revolution in Worship Launched a Global Mission Movement

Matthew Burden

Let the Earth Rejoice: How a Revolution in Worship Launched a Global Mission Movement
© 2026 by Matthew Burden. All Rights Reserved.

No part of this book may be reproduced, stored in a retrieval system, or transmitted in any form or by any means—electronic, mechanical, photocopy, recording, or otherwise—without prior written permission from the publisher, except brief quotations used in connection with reviews. This manuscript may not be entered into or used to train any AI system without the publisher's w ritten consent(permissions@wclbooks.com). For corrections, email editor@wclbooks.com.
For corrections, email editor@wclbooks.com.

William Carey Publishing (WCP) publishes resources to shape and advance the missiological conversation in the world. We publish a broad range of thought-provoking books and do not necessarily endorse all opinions set forth here or in works referenced within this book.

The URLs included in this book are provided for personal use only and are current as of the date of publication, but the publisher disclaims any obligation to update them after publication.

Scripture quotations marked NIV are taken from the Holy Bible, New International Version®, NIV®. Copyright © 1973, 1978, 1984, 2011 by Biblica, Inc.™ Used by permission of Zondervan. All rights reserved worldwide. www.zondervan.com. The "NIV" and "New International Version" are trademarks registered in the United States Patent and Trademark Office by Biblica, Inc.™

Published by William Carey Publishing
10 W. Dry Creek Cir
Littleton, CO 80120 | www.missionbooks.org

William Carey Publishing is a ministry of Frontier Ventures
Pasadena, CA | www.frontierventures.org

Cover and Interior Designer: Mike Riester

ISBNs: 978-1-64508-623-9 (paperback)
978-1-64508-625-3 (epub)

Printed Worldwide

30 29 28 27 26 1 2 3 4 5 IN

Library of Congress Control Number: on file

Contents

Preface

This is the story of how a world-changing movement came to be, a movement that turned Christianity into a truly global religion and reshaped the destiny of entire continents. The wave of Protestant missionaries that went out from Europe and North America at the turn of the nineteenth century opened up an entirely new chapter in the history of the Christian faith. We who live in the aftermath of that movement can sometimes forget just how revolutionary it was. In the words of the historian Meic Pearse, "The launching of the evangelical missionary movement, as much as the fall of the Bastille, was the threshold of the modern age."[1]

Suddenly, a series of new movements erupted from an unexpected corner of English Protestant churches and launched an enterprise that transformed the face of the world. In 1792, William Carey published his famous *Enquiry*, a treatise on the call for global mission. He then helped to found the first modern missionary society and followed that by going himself as a missionary to India. In doing so, an immense wave of activity was stirred up, inspiring representatives from almost every Protestant church to send out missionaries to the farthest ends of the earth.

Where did this startling new movement come from? In many cases, mission histories focus on the work of Carey and his contemporaries, crediting the great missionary and the theologians in his circle, whose ideas, foresight, and courage were instrumental in making the mission movement a reality. Others look a bit further into

1 Pearse, *Age of Reason*, 16.

the past, noting the mid-century stirrings of the Evangelical Revival in England and the Great Awakening in America, or the earlier mission undertakings of the Lutherans and Moravians. Much of the time, though, to emphasize just how revolutionary Carey's mission movement was, popular histories try to offer a clean-cut storyline that puts the spotlight squarely on Carey and his fellow Nonconformists (English Baptists and Congregationalists) at the end of the century. Carey is presented as a figure who said things no one else had thought to say, making a case for global mission that few had ever ventured to make before.

In many ways, Carey deserves to be at the center of the story; he was an epoch-making character on whose work the revolution in world mission turned. Still, it is worth noting that the characterization of history as a sequence of the contributions of great men and women has been shown, repeatedly, to be rather too simplistic. As is almost always the case, there were other factors working in the background—movements of new ideas and fresh conceptions that had been bubbling up beneath the surface for some time, which made possible the favorable reception of Carey's contribution. In short, William Carey's momentous flurry of activity in the 1790s was the culmination of a much longer story that had been developing in the background for quite some time.

I can remember when I was first struck by the incompleteness of the Carey-centered narrative of the Protestant mission movement. It struck me that Carey's work came in the 1790s, and yet I couldn't get the words of an old hymn out of my mind, one that was much older than Carey:

> Jesus shall reign where'er the sun
> Does its successive journeys run;
> His kingdom stretch from shore to shore
> Till moons shall wax and wane no more.

This old familiar hymn was written by Isaac Watts, who was closer to the start of the eighteenth century than to the end. This hymn conjured up clear visions of global Christian mission in my mind, invoking praise for Christ from "people and realms of every tongue" and closing with an expansive vision of global worship: "And Earth repeat the loud amen." How was it, then, that people were singing such a clearly missional hymn long before the mission movement itself came along?

Upon looking it up, I saw that Watts's hymn was published in 1719, as part of a collection that included many other songs with a strikingly global perspective, including the much-beloved "Joy to the World." I also knew that Watts and Carey came from a related context—they were both English Nonconformists, members of the closely aligned groups of Baptists and Congregationalists who stood at the forefront of launching the end-of-century mission movement. But if "Jesus Shall Reign" came in 1719, that meant that William Carey's own churches had been singing deeply missional songs for three-quarters of a century before he wrote his treatise on mission. Those songs even predated the mid-century revivals by well over a decade. It struck me that there must be more to the story, some hidden connection between the explosion of new hymns at the beginning of the eighteenth century and the explosion of missions at the end.

This book will explore that hidden connection, making the case that the introduction of a new form of congregational song in the early eighteenth century was one of the central factors that prepared the way for the mission movement in the 1790s. The hymns of Isaac Watts and Philip Doddridge in particular—and especially Watts's 1719 collection of the *Psalms of David Imitated*—prepared the minds and hearts of Nonconformist Christians for the expansive global vision of William Carey and his contemporaries.

That's not to say that other causes of the mission movement do not have a place in the story. As already mentioned, Carey certainly deserves his share of the historical spotlight, and the mid-century revivals and mission-movement precursors deserve their places of honor in that narrative too. This book merely makes the case that there is another rather important piece of the puzzle that has long gone unnoticed, and that the development of the Protestant mission movement cannot fully be understood without first seeing the growing vision of global mission in the songs that Christians had already been singing for decades.

The research upon which this book rests comes from my doctoral dissertation, representing the fruit of years of study in the intersecting fields of church history, missiology, and liturgics. This research stands alongside my earlier book, *Missionary Motivations* (also from William Carey Publishing), as a contribution to the growing field of historical missiology, which seeks to understand the missiological ideas that informed and motivated earlier generations of Christians, as articulated in their own time. In engaging in this journey of understanding with the church through the ages, we gain insight into our own ways of considering and articulating the missional nature of our faith, as light from the past helps to illuminate the path ahead.

Introduction

Let's begin with a little thought experiment. Imagine the classic analogy of a pond with ripples moving across the surface. A stone is thrown in the center, and the ripples spread out all the way to the edges, affecting every corner of the pond. This is essentially what happened to the global church when a revolution in worship arose in the English-speaking churches of the early 1700s. Then again, a second time, near the end of the same century: another wave is sent out, as a new surge of interest in global missionary endeavors crosses the pond once again.

This is the story of how a small, often-overlooked group of Christians ended up changing the world—not just once, but twice, all in less than a century. Picture, if you will, the Christian world in the eighteenth century: a faith deeply rooted and long established, with its Orthodox, Catholic, and Protestant branches, but with its current growth mostly limited to the territories of a few European nations. Vast swaths of Africa, Asia, and the Pacific remained untouched by the gospel, and Christianity's presence in the Americas was often entangled in colonial ambitions, particularly where the Spanish and Portuguese were involved. Orthodox and Catholic churches had experienced waves of missionary engagement in the past, from monastic missions in the first millennium to the priests who accompanied conquistadors and fur traders in the age of discovery.

The Protestant contribution to world mission, however, was notably lacking, even though two full centuries had passed since the Reformation. There were tiny, isolated steps outward, usually in the overseas colony of some Protestant power, but they were so limited as to make little impact on the vast spiritual needs of the non-Christian world. Then, strangely and suddenly, a few things began happening on the unnoticed fringes of the Protestant world that would turn the established picture entirely on its head.

The little corner of Protestantism that would become the flashpoint of this transformation is familiar to later generations: the pietists, revivalists, and conscientious dissenters who would build the worldwide movement known as Evangelicalism. Their current prominence makes their backstory appear larger than it was, but in the eighteenth century, they were very much in the minority.

There was another strange thing about this group as they approached the decades that would lead them onto the world stage: they didn't sing. At least, not in the way they do today. In the English-speaking Christian world, there had not yet emerged that medium of praise which would later become a vehicle for all the vitality of their faith—the congregational hymn. These were churches where the spoken word reigned, and where singing (if done at all) was a repetition of the same texts that were spoken—the Scriptures, particularly the psalms—often in long and laborious fashion. There was not yet a native liturgy of praise in these churches, through which they could give voice to their own worship alongside the voices of Scripture and tradition.

But in the opening decades of the eighteenth century, that all changed rapidly and dramatically. As a wave of new praises rose and stretched across the Protestant world, something else was stirring in its wake: a growing desire, as yet unarticulated or even unimagined, to send the sound of God's praise to every nation under heaven. A new movement in worship burst out of this tiny segment of eighteenth-century churches and continued until it transformed the worship of Christians all over the world. Just behind that wave, the very same group of churches sparked another movement—the first great Protestant mission movement—which would reshape the face of Christianity and render it a truly global faith.

The same little group, a few marginal English Protestants existing beyond the outskirts of their national church, sent not one but two waves of ripples across the surface of the pond in less than a century. But why should this be? After all, if the pond in the analogy represents the whole Christian world, they were far from the only group throwing pebbles into the water. The eighteenth century was a time of growth, new awakenings, and spiritual vitality for many Christian groups, so why was this one tiny segment of the global church so effective at producing waves that touched every side of the pond in a way that no other contemporary group managed to do? The historian might rightly wonder whether there was some hidden connection between these two movements—whether, in fact, the revolution in hymnody had somehow led to the second wave, the revolution in world mission.

As we consider this question, a different picture begins to emerge—it becomes clear that perhaps the waves are not so much the result of various churches tossing their stones into the water, but of a different source altogether. To have two such waves, starting from the same set of small, unlikely, overlooked denominations, and reaching the farthest edges of the Christian world—and further, to observe that the waves were connected, each creating the way for the other—calls for a deeper explanation. Perhaps it is better to envision these waves as the result of a great wind moving over the surface of the pond, bringing forth the out-rushing ripples of its own accord. Seeing the interconnectedness of these two great movements in global Christian life suggests a work of providence. Here, in this brief window in time in the eighteenth century, we see the Spirit doing again what was done at the beginning, where (as an evocative rendering of the Hebrew might have it) "the Breath of God was blowing gently over the waters" (Gen 1:3, author's translation).

This is, in fact, exactly what we should expect if we have our ears attuned to the way the Spirit has worked in the church throughout the ages. There is an undeniable link between worship and mission, a link that is visible from the earliest days of the church. In the days of the Jerusalem church, the corporate worship of the body of Christ was inextricably tied to its growth (see Acts 2:46–47). When Paul and Barnabas were commissioned to go out on an apostolic mission through Gentile territories, that call emerged from the context of the worship of the Antiochene church (Acts 13:1–3). In Revelation, it is worship that engages the farthest scope of creation, with creatures from every part of the world depicted as praising God (see Rev 5:13; 7:9–10)—a connection between worship and an expansive geographic vision that occurs over and over again in the Bible (most prominently in the Psalms and the prophetic books), and which directly influenced the global-oriented horizons of the Protestant mission movement.

In the years after the New Testament, the same picture holds true. Much of the early expansion of the Christian faith was driven by a pressing concern for the worship of God to be established in new areas, faithful to the vision of Malachi 1:11, which foresaw pure worship being offered to God in every place among the nations. Monastic movements, wandering hermits, and rural bishops took it as their charge to move ever outward onto the fringes of the known world and to establish outposts of God's praise in each new place.[1] Worship was directly linked to mission from the beginning. In that sense, it should come as no surprise that a new movement in worship would lead directly to a new movement in mission; if history is any guide, that seems to be the way the Spirit works among the churches. This is the story of that connection, of how two surprising works of God were linked together in a single set of eighteenth-century churches, and how the effects of those movements changed the world forever.

The Golden Ages of Hymns and Missions

Eighteenth-century England, then, produced two "Golden Ages" that stand as major milestones in the history of Christianity: the Golden Age of Hymns, which began with the work of Isaac Watts in the first decade of the 1700s, and the Golden Age of Protestant Missions,

1 For more on the history of missions in early Christianity and the motivating factors which lay behind its expansion, see Burden, *Missionary Motivations*.

set in motion by William Carey and his contemporaries in the last decade of the same century. While the terminology of a "Golden Age" is historically imprecise (and at times misleading), it is useful in this context, if only to draw attention to the radical nature of the changes that emerged from these new movements in worship and missions. The transformation of congregational song and the launch of a global outreach initiative produced far-reaching effects on many different Christian communions, profoundly shaping both the worship and the geographical scope of the church around the world.

While describing something as a "golden age" is too broad a generalization to be generally useful for academic historical study, these two trends, in hymnody and mission, have been labeled as such in several works of popular history, which points to the dramatic nature of the shifts they represent.[2] Whereas before the early eighteenth century there had been very little use of congregational hymns in the English Protestant tradition (aside from the psalter), they thereafter became a dominant feature of Christian worship across most denominations. Similarly, whereas English Protestant efforts at global mission work had been limited to relatively minor and local efforts, by the nineteenth and twentieth centuries they would become a major feature of Christian outreach, affecting the way that nearly every local church understood its role and swinging the religious history of the global south in new directions. As such, while the history of these movements is too complex for broad generalizations, a case can be made that describing them as golden ages, in light of their impact, is not an overstatement.

Why was the surge in English hymns in the eighteenth century called a golden age? Because it represented a wave that would transform the worship practices in many different languages and denominations, even though it was not the first mover in the story of Protestant congregational hymns. Martin Luther and the Protestants of Germany had been using such hymns since the 1500s. But like the

2 See Norton, "Student Foreign Missions Fellowship," 17; Beeching, *Open Path*, 204; Tucker, *From Jerusalem*, 109–10.

gospel being carried along Roman roads in the ancient world, it was the expansive span of the British Empire that allowed the spark of the hymn revolution to blaze into a conflagration. Throughout the Anglophone world, and then beyond, the singing of congregational hymns transformed and enriched the established patterns of worship for many of the world's Christian denominations.

There were a few minor predecessors in England in the late 1600s, but it was in the early 1700s, with Isaac Watts, that the movement really took off. Watts was the author of innumerable classic hymns, ones we still sing regularly today, some three hundred years later. Here are just a few of Watts's hymns that readers might recognize: "Joy to the World," "Alas and Did My Savior Bleed" ("At the Cross"), "I Sing the Mighty Power of God," "Come We That Love the Lord" ("Marching to Zion"), "O God Our Help in Ages Past," and "When I Survey the Wondrous Cross."

The generations of hymn writers that followed in Isaac Watts's wake—John and Charles Wesley, Philip Doddridge, Augustus Toplady, Anne Steele, John Newton, and William Cowper, just to name a few—were so impressive that the eighteenth century holds an exalted position in the history of hymnody. The list of hymns they contributed to the standard canon of congregational song is staggering. It includes "And Can It Be that I Should Gain," "Christ the Lord is Risen Today," "O For a Thousand Tongues to Sing," "Hark the Herald Angels Sing," "Rejoice, the Lord is King," "O Happy Day," "Rock of Ages," "Dear Refuge of My Weary Soul," "Amazing Grace," and "There is a Fountain." These hymn writers still hold places of honor in the canon of Protestant hymnody three centuries later, and the man who started it all—Isaac Watts—still arguably holds the most prominent position of all.

And what about the so-called Golden Age of Missions? While this is not the most frequent term for referring to the period, an argument can be made that it merits the title (at least in the Protestant world). The period from 1792 to the beginning of the twentieth century can also be referred to as the "Great Century" of Protestant missions.

Though there were predecessors to the Nonconformists' efforts at global mission—including Catholic, Lutheran, and Moravian missions, of which more will be said in chapter 2—the movement launched by William Carey's ministry in the 1790s represented a transformative leap in both form and scale.

The mission societies born from the Baptist and Congregationalist efforts of the 1790s, followed by similar ventures in other denominations, ended up transforming Africa into a majority-Christian continent, spreading the gospel in new ways in Asia, the Americas, and the Pacific, and within two centuries shifting the entire center of Christianity to the global south. Famous missionaries like Joshua Marshman, William Ward, Samuel Marsden, Henry Martyn, Adoniram and Ann Judson, George and Sarah Boardman, and Robert Morrison all went out in the initial wave of the late eighteenth and early nineteenth centuries, reaching places as far-flung as India, New Zealand, Persia, Burma, and China, all within just a handful of years. This also included notable figures from the African-American community, which sent pastors and missionaries like Daniel Coker and Betsey Stockton to the east and the west, from Sierra Leone to Hawaii. Even after the first wave of missionaries had passed on to glory, it was followed in the mid-nineteenth century by an even more famous contingent of missionary laborers, including David Livingstone, J. Hudson Taylor, C. T. Studd, John Paton, and Robert Moffatt.

This book, following established usages, refers to this wave of activity as the Protestant mission movement. It was a broad, disparate, complicated movement, but with several common innovative features, which included (1) the organization of missionary societies and sending agencies, (2) the widespread participation of volunteer laypeople as missionaries, and (3) an institutional disassociation from the official branches of colonial imperialism (in which most previous mission efforts had been entangled). It was a politically independent, church-based wave of volunteer-driven prayer, activism, and giving that encompassed the world, offering a whole new model for the movement of the gospel among the nations. Just as the explosive emergence of congregational hymns in the life of the church can rightly be called a revolution, so too can this new wave of missionary activity.

Studying the Revolutions in Hymnody and Mission

Despite the fact that this English Protestant milieu birthed two golden ages within a single century, very little scholarly work has been done in researching the relationship between these trends in hymnody and mission within their eighteenth-century setting. While both the rise of congregational hymns and the Protestant mission movement have been extensively explored in scholarly literature, they have typically been examined separately. It is important to reiterate that many other factors inspired and led to the launch of the Protestant mission movement, including the enthusiasm of the Evangelical Revival and the Great Awakening in the 1730s and '40s, the example of locally based missionaries like David Brainerd, and the personal genius of visionary leaders like Andrew Fuller and William Carey. There has not yet, however, been a comprehensive examination of the effects of the rising tide of hymnody on the launch of the mission movement.

The emergence of two such golden ages in quick succession is remarkable, but there's an additional surprise: both movements originated from precisely the same group, and an unlikely group at that. A small subset of a marginalized minority in England—known as Nonconformists or Dissenters (in this context, the Baptists and Congregationalists emerged as the most important representatives of the group)—were the source of both the new form of worship and the great wave of mission that erupted from the English-speaking world just a few decades later. This leads to a natural question: Was there a hidden link whereby the effects of the new form of worship positioned the early English Baptists and Congregationalists better than their peers to see the challenge of world evangelization in a new light?

The focus of this book's research is early Nonconformist hymnody, because it was this branch of English Christianity that was responsible for the early impetus in both the hymn-writing and mission movements. Since the Golden Age of Hymns emerged from the efforts of Nonconformists in the first half of the eighteenth century, and the Golden Age of Protestant Missions from Nonconformists in the second half, it is worth asking whether one might discern seeds of the later movement already present in the earlier one. In the nineteenth century that followed, the two movements in hymns and missions overlapped and influenced one another, making it a reasonable conjecture that the early stages of English hymnody may have provided the mission movement with fertile ground for its theological growth.

As it turns out, that is indeed what the data suggest. A comprehensive survey of early Nonconformist hymnody shows a clear and rising arc in the development of missiological themes. More intriguingly, one hymnbook in particular—Isaac Watts's 1719 reimagination of the psalms of David—appears to have offered a unique and original introduction of those missional themes into a church culture that had previously given almost no thought to the task of global mission.

This book, and the research upon which it rests, presents a new argument: that the form of worship popularized by Watts helped to shape the ecclesiastical culture of English Nonconformity toward a greater missional awareness, thus preparing the way for the mission movement that would emerge at the end of the century. In effect, the content of the hymns—and the specific nature of hymns as vehicles for deep theological pedagogy—brought forth something new in the churches that sang them: an awareness and a spirit that had previously been lacking, and that new spirit ultimately produced a wave of missional activity such as the world had never seen before.

The first three chapters of this book will set the stage for understanding this thesis, explaining the historical contexts of the churches, worship movements, and mission movements that weave together to form the narrative of eighteenth-century church life. Chapter 1 will provide a deeper look at the history and background of the group that stands at the center of the story, the Nonconformists (or Dissenters), who were comprised of several marginal English denominations, including the two most important for our purposes in this book: Congregationalists and Baptists. Chapters 2 and 3 lay out the historical background of missions and hymns, respectively, focusing especially on their development in England. These historical chapters provide a thorough background for the subject at hand and will benefit most readers; however, some who find the material challenging and are more inclined to look first at the contributions of Isaac Watts and Philip Doddridge may want to proceed directly to chapter 4 and beyond, which form the central argument of the book.

With chapter 4, the book's focus narrows to its core thesis, introducing the life and work of Isaac Watts. This chapter will argue that—despite the missional contributions of Watts's hymns—Watts himself was surprisingly not a very missional thinker. Chapter 5 then examines the collection of hymns that stands at the center of this story, Watts's 1719 *Psalms of David Imitated*, making the case that its hymns represent a significant new infusion of missional thought into the life of Nonconformist churches. Chapter 6 will look at the life and work of Philip Doddridge in the mid-eighteenth century, whose contributions to the missiological content of English hymns are perhaps just as important as Watts's, though in a rather different way. Whereas Watts's incorporation of the missiology of the Book of Psalms increased the volume and frequency of missional content in hymns, Doddridge's usage was clearer and more intentional. Regarding his vision for the global spread of the Christian faith, Philip Doddridge was a man well ahead of his time.

The final two chapters provide a resolution to the historical narrative and offer suggestions for the contemporary church. Chapter 7 considers the continued intertwining of hymns and missiological content in the latter half of the eighteenth century, including an analysis that connects the missiological themes in the earlier hymns to the same themes as they appear in William Carey's 1792 treatise.

Chapter 8 concludes the book by offering practical applications for the life and worship of the church today.

A few technical notes that the reader would do well to keep in mind: First, some of the spellings and orthography in the primary sources have been updated to make them more accessible to the modern reader; and second, the book can be read in either a broad or a narrow sense, so it is important to know exactly which interpretation of the terms is in play; this is the case with both "mission" and "worship."

The definition of "mission" used in this book rests on the classic foundations of the Protestant mission movement and refers to the cross-cultural dissemination of the Christian faith on a global scale. In modern missiological sources, "mission" can refer either to a specific sense regarding intentional programs of bringing the doctrines and practices of Christianity to various people groups around the world or to a broader, more general sense of the "missio Dei"—that is, anything that could be identified with the mission of God in the world, including local ministry, social justice, development work, and so on. This book does not argue that the latter definition is improper; rather, the broader definition often represents an edifying expansion of how we think about mission. However, one must choose either meaning to be clear about what is communicated. Since this book focuses on the launch of a cross-cultural missionary enterprise aimed at disseminating the Christian faith across global borders, I will be using the former definition. All references to mission(s), missional, or missiology in this book thus carry that narrower sense of the terminology.

The word "worship" also has a broad range of usages. In common parlance, many people today use it to refer to singing songs in a Christian service, often with reference to just one particular style of singing. "Worship" has come to refer to the part of a contemporary service that features guitars and drums, almost to the exclusion of all else. It has even come to carry that meaning beyond the context of church services, becoming a term for a certain genre of Christian music, whether in church or elsewhere.

But this is an unfortunately narrow way of using the term, as worship classically refers to the whole array of activities by which Christians declare the glory of God together. The English term comes from an older form, "worthship"—so one could say, for example, that the angels in the vision from Revelation are ascribing worth-ship to Christ when they say, "Worthy is the Lamb, who was slain, to receive power and wealth and wisdom and strength and honor and glory and praise!" (Rev 5:12 NIV). In this sense, any act is an act of worship if it affirms the *worthiness* of God to be the recipient of our praise and thanksgiving.

Traditionally, then, "worship" referred to the totality of a church gathering, including all the liturgy, prayers, Scripture readings, offerings, and rites. As congregational singing became a more central part of the church service, however, "worship" gradually shifted in popular usage to refer to the sung portion of the service. This shift was perhaps not entirely a matter of chance, as the sung portion of the service closely matched the actions depicted in Revelation's canticles ascribing worth-ship to God.

This book deals with the development of congregational singing, and as such, almost all references to worship will have congregational singing in view. For theological purposes, the broader sense of the term is almost always the better one, applying "worship" to the full scope of Christian actions rendering devotion to God. While acknowledging this, we are bound by certain practical constraints in pursuing our current course of study, and it would become too unwieldy to constantly make distinctions between congregational singing and the other activities in a church service. While there will be occasions where "worship services" might be differentiated from "sung worship" for specificity's sake, readers should assume that any standalone references to worship in this book refer primarily to the communal musical expression of the worth-ship of God in church settings—that is, to congregational singing.

Any readers interested in seeing a scholarly version of this study, including the full dataset, citations, and research methodology, are referred to the author's dissertation, "The Emergence and Development of Missiological Themes in Early Nonconformist Hymnody, 1706–1755."[3]

3 See https://research.sats.ac.za/browse/author.

1

The Unlikeliest Heroes of All

How Nonconformists Led the Charge

To the historian, there's something curious about the story of the emergence of congregational hymns in the English-speaking world. If one were standing at the end of the seventeenth century and were told that a revolution in worship was soon to emerge in England, transforming and enriching the way Christians worshiped on a global scale, a few likely candidates might stand out.

Although Roman Catholic modes of worship were never quick to change or embrace new styles, they certainly had the furthest global reach, so one might think that they could be the locus for a new movement in Christian worship. This had happened before, with the old Ambrosian hymns in the patristic era and the development of Gregorian chant in the medieval world, and Roman Catholicism had recently benefited from a new richness in cross-cultural diversity by making inroads into the Americas. However, Catholicism's impact on English society had been seriously muted ever since the Reformation, and it would not regain a substantial voice there until the mid-nineteenth century.

Another possible candidate would be the Lutheran church, which already had a long history of congregational hymns by the eighteenth century, so one might expect the energizing spark to come from that quarter and illuminate the Anglophone world. But the Lutherans were separated from England by gulfs of language and culture that proved difficult to cross. Even when German-speaking hymn-singing groups emerged in England, their influence was fairly limited.

So one might look to the Anglican church, only recently emerging from the ups and downs of its long experience with the Reformation but possessing transformative potential in its life of liturgical prayer. Anglicans had the strengths of an elegant, beautifully composed prayer book and an insistence that the riches of the daily monastic prayer cycle should be available in every Christian's spiritual life. In the same vein, one might also look to the colonial world, to the forces that were establishing Anglican churches among English settlements on new continents, where the vigor of freshness and cross-cultural interactions might produce something new in the spiritual life of the global church.

But the revolution in worship didn't come from any of these places. In fact, it came from perhaps the least likely candidate of all: a network of tiny, struggling English denominations, just emerging from active persecution and still facing pervasive discrimination from their fellow citizens. They were called Nonconformists (or Dissenters), members of churches that refused to conform to the beliefs and practices of the Anglican state church. Rather than submit to the patterns of worship laid out in the Church of England's *Book of Common Prayer*, they formed their own churches instead. Many of these Nonconformist groups still exist today: Congregationalists (then called Independents), Baptists, Presbyterians, Quakers, and a handful of smaller sects. The Methodists would also be added to the Nonconformists, though somewhat later in the story.[1]

English-speaking Protestantism in the eighteenth century was a dynamic and varied set of movements, but in England it was Anglicanism that still held sway. The Church of England was the dominant denomination by a wide margin, exercising the rights of the established parish system throughout the country. In other parts of the

1 See Richey, "Effects of Toleration," 350; Field, "Counting Religion," 700–704, 710.

British dominions, the picture was a bit more diverse: Presbyterianism reigned in Scotland, and across the ocean in the colonies of New England, it was a dissenting denomination—the Congregationalists—who had seized a role as the dominant form of Christianity there. Adding to this diversity was the fact that there were different streams even within these groups. Cutting across the boundaries of these English denominations were movements defined by their emphases on various principles of piety and practice; among them were the late remnants of the Puritans, high-church and low-church proponents in the established churches, and the nascent evangelical movement.[2]

Within England itself, under the shadow of official state Anglicanism, Nonconformist denominations occupied a precarious role—small and marginalized, yet still present in many communities across the country. Some of their churches elsewhere showed potential for growth (especially in North America, where religious freedom was just beginning to emerge as a hallmark of that society), but in England, the Nonconformists remained partial outcasts in their own towns, and the growth of their churches would never seriously challenge the position of the Anglican state church.

Yet it was this very band of outcasts—and in particular, the Congregationalists and Baptists—who produced a revolution in worship that would transform not only their own churches but would eventually be adopted by the Anglican and Catholic worlds as well. These Nonconformists may have been the unlikeliest candidates of all, yet, in a pattern that has played out many times in the history of God's people, "God has chosen the weak things of this world to shame the strong" (1 Cor 1:27 NIV).

The Emergence of the Nonconformist Churches

To understand the scope of the movements involved, we must first learn a little about where the Nonconformists came from. Their

2 Greaves, "Puritan-Nonconformist Tradition," 449–52; Tapsell, *Later Stuart Church*, 5.

emergence as a movement has its roots in the English Reformation of the sixteenth century, so that is where our story begins.

When King Henry VIII famously severed the Church of England from the Roman Catholic Church because he wanted to annul his marriage, he was unwittingly setting England on a pathway that, at least in some sectors, it had long been prepared to take. Henry's ego was the spark that lit the fuse, but England had seen gradual stirrings of Reformation ideas since well before the Protestant Reformation officially began. England's pre-Reformation roots stretched back two centuries, all the way to John Wycliffe's translation of the Bible in the 1300s and the proto-Protestant preaching of the Lollards that followed.[3]

Several of the most prominent early Reformers, like William Tyndale, were Englishmen active in the Protestant movement well before their country joined the Protestant ranks. Thanks to the new technology of the printing press and the tireless work of Reformation advocates, England was starting to receive Protestant pamphlets and even a few Scripture texts (now available in the people's own language), while Henry VIII—styling himself a champion of Catholicism—initially fought against these forces.[4]

But by the late 1520s, King Henry VIII had switched sides and aligned himself with the Reformation, driven in large part by political motivations. Not only did the break from the Roman Catholic Church allow him to remarry and sustain his hope for a male heir, but it also gave him an opportunity to appropriate an astonishing amount of church property for the crown. Despite the apparent shallowness of his motivations, however, Henry called on the leaders of the English church to shape the English Reformation rather than impose his own whims from the top down. In the clerics' hands, it became something far broader and deeper than mere political reactionism.

3 Shelley, *Church History*, 271–76.

4 See Walker, *History of the Christian Church*, 360–61.

Clergymen like Thomas Cranmer took the reins of the English Reformation, guiding it forward even as it was tugged by changing royal policies over the subsequent decades. The clergy's vision was to reform the English Church so that it aligned with the New Testament and early Christian heritage in doctrine and with long-revered liturgical practices in worship. This was all bound together by a common set of service prayers based on ancient English liturgies and monastic daily offices, thus bringing forth the linchpin of the English Church, the *Book of Common Prayer*.[5]

This transition, however, was anything but smooth. The vast majority of the English were devoted Catholics before Henry VIII's about-face, and many remained so even afterward. Most of the common people, together with the clergy, found themselves caught in the middle. Of the clergy who were sympathetic to Protestant arguments, many simply saw the need for a restoration of balance, a shift back to the New Testament-oriented themes of the early church and the original Catholic witness. Thus two major parties developed in the reaction against medieval Catholicism: one party affirmed the sacramental and liturgical life of the Catholic Church as it had been handed down through tradition and the episcopal hierarchy (but which still saw dangers and errors in other features of medieval Catholic piety), and another party wanted to overturn the whole system and start again from scratch, doing nothing but what the New Testament specifically commanded Christians to do. Despite their differences, both camps generally agreed on one thing, even among the many who still considered themselves Catholic: that reform was needed in the church.

The pendulum of the English Reformation swung back and forth in the mid-1500s due to a few factors, not least of which was the succession crisis that brought Henry's Catholic daughter, Mary, to the throne, where she enacted a vengeful reign of terror against Protestant

5 Davies, *Worship and Theology*, 20.

leaders (thus her famous epithet, Bloody Mary). She was succeeded by her Protestant sister Elizabeth, who switched everything back around again in the Reformers' favor. Both sides counted numerous martyrs in the process, and in the end a new form of Protestantism, one rather different from the continental churches, emerged on England's isle.[6]

While events moved rapidly on the ground, the theological transition was gradual. After the break with Rome that launched the English Reformation, an indigenous Protestant movement began to blossom within just a couple of decades, eventually evolving into its own self-consciously robust version of Protestant catholicity in the seventeenth century.[7] Anglicanism—that form of Christianity that arose from the English Reformation—sought to capture both the Protestant reclamation of Paul's gospel of grace and, at the same time, a reinvigorated patristic heritage that grounded itself in the councils and practices of the early church. It aimed to hold onto those elements of early and medieval Catholic culture that were not forbidden by the spirit and teaching of the New Testament (and thus considered permissible), rather than throwing the proverbial baby out with the bathwater as some minimalist Reformers did. Advocates of Anglicanism celebrated it as a *via media*, a middle way between Catholics and Protestants.

Whether Anglicanism truly achieved its status as a *via media* remains a topic of debate today, but it certainly managed to infuriate, in nearly equal measure, two opposing factions in its own ranks.[8] On one side were those who believed that the English Reformation had gone too far and was in danger of losing the sacramentalism they viewed as the heart of true Christian worship. On the other side were those who felt that the English Reformation hadn't gone nearly far enough and wanted to clear out anything that even vaguely hinted at medieval

6 See Spinks, *Liturgy*, 492–503.

7 Buschart, *Exploring Protestant Traditions*, 115–16; see also Shelley, *Church History*, 312.

8 Simpson, *Puritanism*, 2.

superstition. This latter group, more inclined to the positions which continental Reformed and Anabaptist churches had taken, gradually aligned in the Puritan movement.[9] The Puritans hoped to cleanse the English church of what they perceived as Catholic accretions in the liturgy and to reform the habits and manners of English life in a more pietistic direction.

Throughout the early seventeenth century, the Puritan movement flourished and diversified. Many Puritans chose to remain within the Anglican church, advocating for further reforms in doctrine and practice. But many others decided to leave the established church and form their own congregations centered around theological opinions of particular importance to them.[10] Those convinced that an episcopal hierarchy was an unbiblical form of church polity formed the churches that would come to be known as Presbyterian and Congregational (the latter often referred to as "Independent" in early sources), while those who believed that infant baptism was an unbiblical practice separated themselves into various Baptist associations (in this latter case, contacts with continental theology also provided a formative influence). These groups, together with Quakers, became known as Dissenters, in that they dissented from the mainstream doctrine and practice of the Anglican church.[11]

Within those who remained with the Church of England, the opposing camps of high-church traditionalists and low-church Puritans each experienced a series of rises and falls in their influence until the climactic events of the English Civil War in the mid-1600s. The Civil War cut along political and religious fault lines, and Oliver Cromwell's volatile interregnum of the 1650s saw power resting briefly in Puritan hands.

The Puritan ascendancy was not to last, however, and the traditionalist wing, led by the monarchy, reasserted itself. After the

9 Steinmetz, *Reformers in the Wings*, 144–45; Olson, *Story of Christian Theology*, 495–96.

10 See Spinks, *Liturgy*, 503–8; Noll, *History of Christianity*, 32–35.

11 Richey, "Effects," 350.

Civil War and the Cromwellian protectorate, life became more difficult for Puritans and dissenters from the Church of England. Puritanism (and religious dissent more broadly) was now associated in many people's minds with the chaos and violence of the recent upheaval. With the restoration of the Stuart monarchy in 1660, official policy was much more wary of any further Puritan influence in church life and politics, and the place of Puritanism within the Anglican tradition declined.[12] David Hume captured the spirit of many later Englishmen when he referred to the Puritanism of the Cromwellian protectorate as "wretched fanaticism."[13]

When political power returned to the monarchy with the Restoration, the Puritans were on the outside looking in, blamed for the entire national catastrophe. The crown now had a significant interest in keeping Puritan influences in check, and in 1662, alongside a new edition of the *Book of Common Prayer* (which excised some Puritan positions), all clergy in England were required to submit to the Act of Uniformity. This legislation required the clergy to swear an oath of conformity, agreeing to lead worship according to the standards and practices enjoined in the revised *Book of Common Prayer*. That was problematic, because not only had the 1662 prayer book swung back toward high-church interests, it also included liturgical references celebrating the political defeats of earlier Dissenters.[14] The Act of Uniformity was the legal death knell of Puritanism in the Anglican church. More than two thousand ministers refused to swear the oath of conformity and were ejected from Anglican clerical orders. These expelled clerics—perhaps a fifth of the entire clergy of England's state church—were henceforth known, together with their followers, as Nonconformists.[15]

---

12 Tapsell, *Later Stuart Church*, 2; see also Spurr, "Later Stuart Puritanism," 89–107.

13 Quoted in Seed, *Dissenting Histories*, 78.

14 Seed, 88–90; Deacon, *Philip Doddridge*, 22.

15 Bready, *England*, 21; see also Calamy *Abridgement*; *Continuation*.

Though Puritanism had never really sought separation from the Church of England, that result had been thrust upon it, and the new ex-Anglican Nonconformists joined the ranks of the small, fledgling Dissenting denominations that had already established a life and presence of their own. Baptist churches and Quaker meetings had been living a semi-persecuted existence in the shadows for some time, and now a new wave of ousted Puritans joined the rising tide of Nonconformism, with most of the gains accruing to Presbyterian and Congregationalist churches.

Nonconformists at the Turn of the Eighteenth Century

The Nonconformists were not a unified group, but a collection of individuals who dissented from the mandated practices of the Church of England. Each of the Nonconformist churches had its own story and historical development, branching out from the vibrant, many-fruited tree of the Protestant Reformation.

There were Presbyterians, heirs of John Calvin's wing of the Reformation, who in Scotland had risen to such heights as to become the state church. In England, however, they had ridden the turbulent ups and downs of the Civil War and ended up out of favor in the aftermath. English Presbyterians, although major representatives of the Nonconformists, were not primary players in either the move toward hymns or missions. The early eighteenth century was a period of doctrinal rifts in their church culture, and in their practices of worship, they tended to favor either no singing or the exclusive use of psalmody. Congregational hymns were viewed as unfit for the worship of God, being merely "men's composures" as opposed to the inspired words of Scripture.[16]

The Quakers (or Friends) were another major group in the mix of Nonconformism, a branch of the English Reformation that had grown in a more radical direction than its contemporaries. Known for their

16 Foote, *Three Centuries*, 150; Parker, "Hymn," 398; Templeton and Riglan, *Reforming Worship*, 24–25.

early emphasis on ecstatic manifestations and personal revelations from God, they gradually developed into a more subdued form, where a deep-rooted spirituality, marked by prayer and silence, was key. As such, with silence at its core, it also did not play a role in the revolution in hymnody.[17]

The two other main players on the Nonconformist stage, however, were at the forefront of both new movements in hymnody and mission: Congregationalists and Baptists. Congregationalists were among the leading heirs of the Puritan tradition and had already established a semi-independent life as a denomination through their North American branch, which had been serving as the state church of the Massachusetts Bay Colony. Congregationalists, as their name implies, were organized around a belief in congregational polity and a rejection of ecclesiastical hierarchies, but this does not mean that they were all independent, nondenominational churches in the modern sense: rather, they were deeply connected to one another and to the international communion between English and American churches. It was partly this transoceanic nature of the Congregationalist communion that positioned it to be a leader in the coming revival of the 1730s, known as the Great Awakening in the North American colonies and as the Evangelical Revival in England (though in the Congregationalists' case, their involvement with revivalism was much more pronounced in the American movement than in the English one).[18]

The Baptists were a movement that had arisen early in the 1600s, heirs of a diverse theological heritage that sprang from the English Reformation and also included inspiration from continental Anabaptists.[19] Like the Congregationalists, they favored local, congregational polity rather than ecclesiastical hierarchy, but they went further by also disavowing infant baptism. By baptizing only

17 See Davies, *Worship and Theology*, 94, 126–27; Benson, *English Hymn*, 88; Watts, *Dissenters*, 312.

18 O'Brien, "Transatlantic Community," 813.

19 See Bushart, *Exploring Protestant Traditions*, 146.

believers old enough to make their own faith commitments, Baptists radically changed the idea of church membership. To be a member of the church necessitated a visible commitment to living out one's Christian faith, not merely a status one has held since infancy.[20]

This made the Baptist model, in contrast to Anglicanism or Congregationalism, one that could not operate as a state church. Whereas an established church could view all its members, from infants to adults, as a single category overlapping with their status as citizens of their society, Baptist membership did not completely overlap with civic membership. Rather, the Baptist view necessarily encouraged people to see matters of church and state as oriented toward separate realms—a perspective that would significantly impact not just religious thought but also political practice over the subsequent centuries.

For the purposes of this study, the differences between Baptists and Congregationalists are not substantial. Both were heirs to a relatively low-church, Puritan-inspired form of worship, and their Sunday meetings would have looked similar. Both placed similar emphases on the preaching of Scripture and had similar patterns of prayer and congregational song. Baptists were the first to incorporate the new style of congregational hymns into their worship, led by a few English churches in the 1690s. However, it was the Congregationalists who popularized the hymn and spread the influence of this new form far and wide.[21] In regard to hymns, there was a greater degree of mutual usage between Baptists and Congregationalists throughout the eighteenth century than between most other denominations.

While the Baptists did not have as significant an international presence in the colonies as the Congregationalists, they were represented there on a small scale and shared in the eighteenth-century revivals on both sides of the Atlantic. Other groups at the center of the revival, like the Methodists, would go on to have an enormous

20 See Maring and Hudson, *Baptist Manual*, 45–46.

21 See Wallace, *Shapers of English Calvinism*, 27; Benson, *English Hymn*, 106.

impact on English Christianity, but in the eighteenth century, they were not yet recognized as a Nonconformist denomination in their own right (still maintaining their roots within Anglicanism). Thus the Methodists initially shared only minimal cross-pollination with other Nonconformist groups.

In the 1660s, when Nonconformism first emerged as a recognizable category of churches, the revivals of the 1730s were still a distant reality. Early Nonconformism faced resistance at almost every level of society. Even though the days of burning schismatics at the stake were now past, being a Nonconformist meant taking a stand of conscience that came with severe social penalties, and, in the case of clergy, occasional imprisonment.[22] For more than two decades after the Act of Uniformity, the English parliament continued to introduce new legislation aimed at restricting the ability of Nonconformists to meet for worship. Nonconformists were prohibited from holding public meetings, and pastors were forbidden from coming within five miles of their parishes. Even lay Nonconformists were barred from the normal avenues of social prestige: ineligible to attend schools like Oxford or Cambridge, restricted from holding political office, and subject to fines, taxes, and double tithes.[23]

These restrictive measures remained in place, to varying degrees, until the Act of Toleration in 1689. That act followed the so-called Glorious Revolution, in which a Dutch Calvinist ruler, William of Orange (the son-in-law of the reigning English king), was invited to claim the throne of England from other members of the royal family, who had been inclined toward fostering a slow drift back towards Catholicism. Even after the Act of Toleration, however, Nonconformists did not have true freedom of worship, and both their clergy and parishioners remained under severe restrictions that waxed and waned with the tumultuous changes in their political

---

22 Tapsell, *Later Stuart Church*, 199–200; cf. Bulman, *Anglican Enlightenment*, 279; Beynon, *Isaac Watts: His Life*, 12.

23 Sell, *Dissenting Histories*, 263.

fortunes. As historian Brian Spinks notes, "the price of Dissent for most was marginalization from the centre of civic and cultural life, with the constant threat of their neighbors' wrath during times of unrest."[24] Nonconformists remained only a small portion of English society, maintaining a constant awareness of their marginal position in standing against the majority. By 1715, they numbered about a quarter of a million people out of a population of five and a half million (amounting to less than 5 percent), about two-thirds of whom were Presbyterians.[25]

Since Nonconformism had arisen from this milieu of social turmoil, driven by issues of local faith and practice, these issues continued to be the main emphasis of many Nonconformist churches throughout the period. Doctrines like congregational polity and believer's baptism became matters of utmost importance for many Christians, convictions they had to hold at the cost of tremendous social repercussions for themselves and their families. Consequently, the apologetic defense of these doctrines formed the primary outward-facing programs of Nonconformist churches.[26]

The broad, nationally focused programs of Puritan reform in the mid-seventeenth century had been repudiated by the British establishment, and Nonconformists were now a minority forced into a defensive posture. Their primary goal was survival and the right to meet for worship, and they did not yet have the practical means to consider a broad, intentional, and organized program of global evangelization.[27] This defensive posture can be seen, for example, in some of the hymns of Benjamin Keach, a Baptist pastor serving in London in the 1690s. Consider this selection from his 1691 hymn, "The Lord, He Is Our Sun and Shield":

24 Spinks, *Liturgy*, 84.

25 Armstrong, *Church of England*, 35; cf. Watts, *Dissenters*, 270; Field, "Counting Religion," 696–97.

26 Richey, "Effects of Toleration," 350–51.

27 See Bready, *England*, 373; Porter, *Religion versus Empire*, 28.

The Lord, he is our sun and shield,
Our buckler and safeguard,
And hence we stand, and will not yield,
Though enemies press hard.

Like as a shield the blow keeps off
The enemy lays on,
So thou keeps off all hurt from us,
And saves us every one.[28]

Not only were the Nonconformists persecuted, they were also fragmented. There was a pronounced local and parochial nature to Nonconformist church life during this period. One can only speak of "the Nonconformist movement" in the broadest terms of theological affinities; for most Nonconformists, their experiences were centered around their own local church or chapel, and thus their outlook tended to be parochial. It would not be until the latter half of the eighteenth century that English society began to develop features allowing for national associations and societies based on particular interests.[29]

All that to say: the Nonconformists who emerged from the seventeenth and into the eighteenth century were not bold, globally minded paragons of missional thinking. They were small, disparate bands of Christians, holding fast to doctrines that their consciences had convinced them were necessary to biblical faith, and seeking above all to survive, persevere, and continue worshiping in their appointed way. They were isolated and insular, focusing above all on simply being able to maintain their convictions and their way of life. Nonconformists were primarily focused on local issues. As such, a strong emphasis on Christian outreach beyond the bounds of Britain did not emerge until the eighteenth century was well underway. Historians have noted that it would be hard to pick a less likely candidate for the genesis of a global mission movement than

28 Keach, *Spiritual Melody*, 32.

29 Tilly, *Popular Contention*, 5–8.

eighteenth-century Nonconformism, which was "an inward-looking sect in an insular nation in an unstable continent."[30]

Still, there were early signs that some new movements were brewing beneath the surface. At the turn of the eighteenth century, Nonconformists were coming out of a period of repression that had specifically targeted their ability to gather for Sunday worship. As a result, the weekly service of Sunday worship took on paramount importance in their lives. The edicts finally lifted by the 1689 Act of Toleration had left their mark: the Conventicle Act, which forbade gatherings of more than five people from different families for worship, and the Five-Mile Act, which acted as a restraining order to keep pastors away from their congregations. Nonconformist congregational life had been forced to exist in the shadows during the three decades of the 1660s, '70s, and '80s.[31] By the time the Act of Toleration restored their ability to meet for public worship in the 1690s, a psychological shift had taken root regarding the surpassing preciousness of congregational worship. The worship of the gathered congregation was not something taken for granted, and it now stood as the absolute focal point for the communal experience of both Baptists and Congregationalists.

It is no surprise, then, that the transformation that would launch them into mission came from that very context, arising out of the gathered worship of the people of God. Starting in the 1690s, a few Baptist pastors began composing new hymns. That in itself was not novel, since there had been a few hymn-writers active in England before that time. But the innovation lay in the hymns' usage: whereas earlier hymns were written as devotional poems for private use, Nonconformists started introducing them into the public worship of their congregations.[32] It was also in the 1690s that a young man named Isaac Watts, still a teenager, tried his hand at writing a new

30 Stanley, *History of the Baptist Missionary Society*, 3.

31 See Deacon, *Philip Doddridge*, 22; Tapsell, *Later Stuart Church*, 199–200.

32 See Wallace, *Shapers of English Calvinism*, 27.

hymn for his Congregationalist church. The same young man, only a decade later, would publish the first landmark hymnbook in English history, and Nonconformist worship would never be the same again.

2

Your Great Commission We'll Proclaim

The Rise of Protestant Missions

Now that we have the main players of the story in view, the next step is to examine the two major movements that arose in the eighteenth century and how they intertwined: the Protestant mission movement and the rise of a new form of English hymnody. The story of the Protestant mission movement is generally well known, at least in its broad outlines. While this book focuses on the 1790s as a watershed moment in the history of mission, the beginnings of a global Protestant wave of missionary activity were already underway well before that date.

This chapter will examine the roots of the mission movement from the Reformation of the 1500s to its launch under William Carey in the 1790s. Although a broad span of history is in view here, it is helpful to remember that our period of greatest interest—the hymnographic revolution of Isaac Watts—occurs some three-quarters of a century before the climax, in the early decades of the 1700s, and thus precedes both the revivals of the Great Awakening and the missionary ventures of the Moravians.

Early Influences

The sixteenth and seventeenth centuries witnessed an astonishing expansion of Roman Catholicism around the world, from Latin

America to India to China, and the Protestants of Europe beheld this surge with a mixture of awe and trepidation. With the efforts of Jesuits, Dominicans, and ordinary priests, Roman Catholicism leapt from being a European faith into a global one in relatively short order. This expansion followed the expeditions of explorers from Catholic countries, with Catholic emissaries accompanying navigators and conquistadors throughout the age of discovery, planting churches, missions, and encomiendas as they went. Within a couple of centuries, Catholicism had been imported and established across the vast Spanish empire, from the Americas to the Philippines, and wherever Portuguese and French traders set up their posts, including Brazil, Africa, India, China, and Canada.[1]

Nonconformist churches were broadly aware of this global Catholic expansion. Their attitudes toward these developments mirrored general English sentiments. The world-encompassing spread of Roman Catholicism was regarded by English Christianity with fear and resentment, sometimes mixed with a grudging sense of awe at the accomplishment. The spirit of the Protestant Reformation was still fresh enough that it was nearly unanimous in England that the Catholic missionary enterprise was a bad thing. Far from believing that indigenous groups around the world were being converted to the Christian faith, most Nonconformists regarded their conversion to Catholicism as merely the exchange of one state of benightedness for another.[2]

Anglicans likewise perceived global Catholic expansion as an imminent political threat on the international stage, a threat that might very well impact England with deadly consequences. Fears of Catholic political subterfuge, regularly stoked in England throughout the seventeenth century, led many English citizens to regard the global reach of Catholicism as a circumstance that might, if left unchecked, lead to Catholics attempting to overthrow the state.[3] Thus, while

1 See Tucker, *From Jerusalem*, 43–66; Neill, *History of Christian Missions*, 177–209.

2 See, for example, Carey, *Enquiry*, 34.

3 See Massie, *Royal Stuarts*, 163, 258–64.

much of England regarded the missionary achievements of the Roman Catholic Church as impressive, they did not view it as an example of true Christian evangelism, and it was generally not drawn upon as inspiration for English missionary efforts.

Nevertheless, the Catholic global expansion was not wholly without benefit for Protestant missions. The Catholic surge across the world went hand in hand with the promotion of knowledge about the lands they visited. Suddenly, whole new continents were laid before the European imagination, and other places long shrouded in mystery and fable—Africa, India, China—were now at the center of the world stage. For each of these regions, from the Americas to East Asia, Protestants in northern Europe became aware of many hundreds of cultures, languages, and ethnicities that had no exposure to the gospel. Some individuals from these distant and disparate cultures even started popping up in the streets of London and other Protestant cities (often via slavery or trade), making their plight impossible to ignore. The perspective of English Christians began to shift, moving from simply having an idea of faceless "heathen" nations beyond their borders to seeing the faces and hearing the stories of those very people. Europe was a society united by numerous lines of communication, and the growing knowledge about the world's peoples—brought in by Spanish, Portuguese, French, and Dutch colonial expansion, as well as England's own growing experience of the slave trade—broadened the perspective of England's residents to include ideas and concerns beyond their local horizons.[4] This new awareness of the world at large, wrought by the age of discovery, was the necessary first step toward launching a Protestant mission movement.[5]

That awareness was also being facilitated, in ever-growing measure, by England's own international ambitions. The emerging political realities of colonialism and global trade were beginning to turn the English mindset toward a more global perspective. Beginning

4 See Marshall, *Making and Unmaking*, 25–40.

5 Marshall, *Making and Unmaking*, 13; Kaul, *Eighteenth-Century British Literature*, 7–15.

with the reign of Elizabeth I in the second half of the sixteenth century, England began to make a slow ascent toward becoming a global power. This was a new and somewhat surprising development for the isolated island kingdom, and for much of the next two centuries, they lagged behind other regional powers in colonization and trade. Spain had taken an early and dominant lead, and other European nations like the Netherlands were often far in advance of the English position.

The rise of English influence on a global scale was aligned with their progress in becoming a naval power, a process that began with the defeat of the Spanish Armada in 1588 and continued through the seventeenth and eighteenth centuries. As naval power expanded, bringing with it investment in infrastructure for seaports and shipbuilding, global trade became a significant aspect of English national life.[6] Even before England's leaders had resolved on becoming a colonizing power, the country aggressively pursued influence in trade, resulting in footholds in the Americas, Africa, and India. Distant nations suddenly became living realities in the English imagination.

England's religious divisions also played an important role in colonial developments. Persecution against Nonconformists spurred emigration and led to the founding of several North American colonies, including Plymouth Colony (Puritan Separatists), Massachusetts Bay Colony (Puritan Congregationalists), Rhode Island Colony (Baptists), and Pennsylvania (Quakers). These American Nonconformists often maintained close communication with congregations back in England, and their experiences with the indigenous populations of North America became well known. The influence of these experiences shaped Nonconformist missiological thought in several directions, though not always positively—for example, they reinforced an early sense that "heathen" populations were resistant to the gospel.[7] By the middle decades of the eighteenth century, however, concurrent with the revolution in hymnody, some

6 Kaul, *Eighteenth-Century British Literature*, 6–7.

7 See Tucker, *From Jerusalem*, 84.

efforts aimed at the conversion of indigenous populations were finding success, and news of these results played a significant role in shifting Nonconformist missiological thought.

Despite these influences encouraging a more global perspective, Nonconformist thought remained highly insular at the turn of the eighteenth century. There were significant challenges and roadblocks, both social and theological, that hindered the development of a missional vision for global engagement. Nonconformist churches of this period were often viewed by later generations as "lacking an evangelical, missionary understanding of the ministry,"[8] ecclesiastical communions in which "mission overseas remained unthinkable to all but the most visionary."[9]

Challenges and Obstacles

Given the new reality in which European Christians suddenly found themselves in the sixteenth and seventeenth centuries, why did it take until the end of the eighteenth century to organize and launch a coordinated effort at global evangelization? There were a significant number of roadblocks to surmount along the way: challenges in the social, national, and theological realms.

First, the sixteenth century was consumed by Protestantism's struggle to separate from Rome and sustain an independent existence. Indeed, one could argue that it wasn't until the mid-seventeenth century—at the Peace of Westphalia and the end of the so-called "Wars of Religion"—that the Protestant churches of northern Europe had the space to look beyond their initial focus on survival, establishment, and security. Only at the end of the seventeenth century did German-speaking regions of Europe experience any kind of reprieve from the near-constant warfare of previous generations. Similarly, England's Protestant Reformation had taken shape in a wild series of back-and-forth swings in the mid-1500s, only to continue tumbling into

8 Richey, "Effects of Toleration," 358.

9 Stanley, *History of the Baptist Missionary Society*, 3.

repeated tension (and, at times, all-out chaos) until the Glorious Revolution of 1688. Given the sheer scope and scale of the political and social challenges facing Protestants in the first two centuries of their existence, it comes as little surprise that much of their thinking was inward-facing, seeking stability and cohesion, rather than developing an outward-facing program of sending emissaries to the nations.[10]

Second, early efforts at mission largely followed the contours of national colonial expansion. Until trade routes and colonies were established for England, Germany, the Netherlands, and other Protestant powers, it would have been nearly impossible to organize a missionary expedition around the world. No captain or investor would be likely to give up his ship for such a scheme. Rather, missionaries' activities had to wait until their country's own ships were already plying the seas, making it much easier to book passage on a trading voyage and establish a mission launch point in an overseas colony. Spain and Portugal (and to some degree, France)—the major Catholic colonial powers—had a significant jump-start on the Protestant states in this regard. It would take until well into the 1600s for England's overseas colonial program to gain much traction, and the German states did not become a major colonial power until nearly the end of the 1800s.

Third, much of Protestantism was skeptical about the prospect of world mission in its early days. That's not to say that all Protestants regarded the idea warily. But the truth is that even if anyone gave any thought to global mission (and many simply did not), there were several entrenched theological ideas that mitigated against it.

One of these ideas, which held greater sway on John Calvin's side of the Reformation than on Martin Luther's, was the belief that God's sovereignty was ordered in such a way that human plans for taking intentional action—such as launching a mission organization—were at best redundant, and at worst, a mark of distrust in the divine timing of God's plan. Not all Calvinist thinkers held this to be true, of

10 See Richey, "Effects of Toleration," 350–51; Bready, *England*, 373; Porter, *Religion versus Empire*, 28.

course—many would have acknowledged intentional human actions as being an ordained means by which God's sovereign plan would be enacted. But this emphasis on the divine plan often had the effect, even unintentionally, of under-emphasizing human agency, and it produced a doctrinal drag effect on the process of launching mission movements.[11]

Calvinist theology was a predominant influence across much of the Puritan movement, and this carried over into Nonconformism. While not the case with Quakers or General Baptists, a strong form of Calvinism constituted the theological bedrock of most Congregationalists, Particular Baptists, and Presbyterians. Once the drag effect of its overwhelming insistence on divine sovereignty found a more active interpretation, Calvinists became some of the most effective leaders of the global mission movement. However, in the seventeenth and early eighteenth centuries, the inertial resistance of that doctrinal model was still in play. In fact, it exercised significant influence in Nonconformist circles until the 1780s and '90s, when it first began to see a reversal with the theological work produced by Andrew Fuller and William Carey, Baptists with a view toward global mission.[12]

It should also be noted that the predominance of Calvinist theology did not suppress all missiological ideas in early Nonconformism, as it was within those same theological circles that the optimistic global vision of postmillennial eschatology grew and flourished.[13] Postmillennialism held that the nations would be converted to the Christian faith on a massive scale before the Second Coming of Christ. While that might seem like a fruitful theological foundation for building a mission movement, the reality is that early postmillennialists were often content to believe that the nations would be converted but did not take the next step of believing that it might be

11 See Lambert, *Inventing the "Great Awakening"*, 26–28; Crawford, "Origins," 373.

12 Chute, Finn, and Hayken, *Baptist Story*, 102–104; Stanley, *History of the Baptist Missionary Society*, 5.

13 Kidd, *Great Awakening*, 8; Bosch, *Transforming Mission*, 284.

through their own actions that this conversion would occur, resulting in a lack of resolution to be directly involved in global evangelization.

An example of this optimistic eschatological hope, held without any corresponding sense of practical action toward such goals, comes from Isaac Watts's reaction to hearing about the revivals breaking out in New England in the late 1730s: "These [revivals] are certainly little specimens of what Christ and his grace can do when he shall begin to revive his own work and to spread his Kingdom thro' the earth . . . I adore his good pleasure and rejoice, but wait for the blessing in European countries."[14] Nonconformist Calvinists of this type believed that the nations would be converted but felt content to leave it up to the timing of God's sovereignty as to when that would happen, often giving no thought to taking any action themselves.[15] (As later chapters will show, Watts's richly missiological hymns still lack a sense of responsibility and intentionality toward missional action, likely for this reason.)

Another theological idea that tended to diminish any surge of enthusiasm for global mission was the model of biblical interpretation that had developed around the Great Commission. For Christians today, it seems strange that anyone could have such deep familiarity with the New Testament as the early Protestants did, and yet still not see a pressing mandate for global evangelization. After all, it's right there—at the end of the Gospel of Matthew, in the "long ending" of Mark, and at the beginning of Acts—Jesus explicitly telling his followers to go out and proclaim his gospel to all nations, even to the very ends of the earth. How could they read such passages, prominently featured as the closing and opening sections of major books of the New Testament, and yet not consider how they might obey Jesus's command?

The answer to this question, which surprises many modern readers, is that most Christians in previous centuries did not assume

14 Quoted in Kidd, *Great Awakening*, 21.

15 Kidd, *Great Awakening*, 8; Klauber and Manetsch, *Great Commission*, 89–90.

that the Great Commission passages were written to them. Rather, the assumption was that Jesus was speaking solely to his own disciples, the ones he was sending out as apostles to the nations. This was the dominant reading of the Great Commission in the early church.[16] For the first five centuries of church history, no one (with the solitary exception of good old Saint Patrick) viewed the Great Commission as a command directed at themselves. It was assumed to be the disciples' commission they fulfilled during their first-century missionary labors. As Cyril of Scythopolis put it in the sixth century:

> Accordingly, when [Jesus] sent out his disciples for the salvation of our race, he said, "Go and teach all nations, baptizing them in the name of the Father and of the Son and of the Holy Spirit." On receiving this teaching, they sped through the whole world to proclaim piety by both word and deed . . . This is why the knowledge of God has risen upon the world; . . . this is why from all nations flocks of holy martyrs have sprung up.[17]

That was the prevailing thought throughout much of church history, and it still held considerable sway in some early Protestant readings of those texts: Jesus gave his commission to his disciples, and they fulfilled it. As we'll see, even Isaac Watts appears to have understood the Great Commission in this way. To give another example from the heart of the Reformation itself: John Calvin's commentary on Matthew's Great Commission passage treats it as the apostolic ordination of the eleven disciples, with no apparent ongoing application to subsequent generations of Christians. Calvin writes, "when Christ appeared to the disciples, he likewise commissioned them to be apostles, to convey into every part of the world the message of eternal life."[18]

16 Green, *Evangelism*, 239; Louth, "Church's Mission," 650.

17 Binns, *Cyril of Scythopolis*, xvi–xix.

18 Water, *Parallel Classic Commentary*, 420.

As we will see, both of these theological challenges—related to the sovereignty of God and the interpretation of the Great Commission—remained relevant throughout much of the eighteenth century, even as the groundwork was being laid for the mission movement in other parts of English Protestant life.

Early Efforts at Global Mission

Despite the challenges posed above, there were some early Protestant efforts to launch a global mission movement. These tended to be small-scale and uncoordinated, but they are notable for their clear-eyed view of the necessity of mission and their courage in undertaking it. The most significant early movers on the Protestant side came from the continental churches, notably the Lutherans and the Dutch Reformed.

The Dutch were one of the few Protestant powers active in the first wave of colonial expansion, though their global colonial presence tapered off significantly in later periods. As early as 1620, the Dutch East India Company had a missionary hard at work in their colonial possessions (present-day Indonesia). Churches were established in Batavia (now Jakarta) and on outlying islands, but the progress of the mission was hindered by resistance from local colonial officials.[19]

The Lutherans, sponsored by the king of Denmark, established a missionary post at Tranquebar, a newly acquired Danish possession in India, in 1706. This mission, while limited in scope by the small number of workers and by resistance from Danish colonial officials, nevertheless secured a landmark achievement: the translation and publication of the Bible in the Tamil language.[20]

In concert with these initial movements by continental Protestants, the Anglican church began to inch toward developing a mission program in the early 1700s. The first such group, the Society for the Propagation of Christian Knowledge (SPCK), would later expand into cross-cultural missionary labors but was more focused on

19 See Kidd, *Great Awakening*, 8.

20 Robert, *Converting Colonialism*, 28–29.

ministries internal to England during the first century of its activity. The second group, the Society for the Propagation of the Gospel in Foreign Parts (SPG), was the first Anglican society specifically devoted to global mission. While the title of the SPG suggests that it may have been involved in cross-cultural missionary work, its dominant aim was actually the establishment of Anglican churches for British colonists overseas.[21] In the words of historian John Hull, it was "mainly confined to the provision of chaplaincies to overseas colonies and trading posts."[22]

The SPG's charter refers to ministry efforts among British subjects but makes no mention of the evangelization of indigenous peoples or slaves. Its work throughout the first century of its existence was confined to British colonies, and within those colonies, its overriding aim was to provide well-trained clergy and functioning churches for the colonists.[23] Cross-cultural missionary efforts, where present, were minimal at best, remained within the bounds of British territories, and were often viewed with suspicion by British administrative authorities and even by Anglican officials themselves. In the few early instances where attempts at cross-cultural evangelism appear to have been intended, the record is one of overall silence, marked here and there by the failure of missionaries to make the efforts that were asked of them.[24]

Nevertheless, the work of the SPG formed yet another channel of experience that brought a broader perspective back to the churches of England, and its labors helped raise awareness of the religious state of various nations around the world and their potential needs for action and assistance. Even so, it was not until the 1770s and 1780s, with the

21 Marshall, *Making and Unmaking*, 40.

22 Hull, "Isaac Watts," 75; see also Robert, *Converting Colonialism*, 6; Goodall, *History of the London Missionary Society*, 1.

23 Porter, *Religion versus Empire*, 17–18; Etherington, *Missions and Empire*, 41–42; Stanley, *Bible and the Flag*, 55.

24 Neill, *Colonialism and Christian Missions*, 14; Bickham, *Savages within the Empire*, 212–13.

publication of accounts of Captain Cook's global circumnavigation, that the condition of indigenous populations around the world fully captured the British public imagination.[25] This growing sense of global awareness, initially slow and inchoate, would ultimately form a core part of William Carey's presentation of the need for world mission in his 1792 treatise.

In each of these outreaches by Protestant powers in the seventeenth and early eighteenth centuries, a few repeated themes emerge. First, these attempts were largely content to be a constituent part of the colonial enterprise. They were sanctioned by official national bodies and rode the coattails of their nations' colonial establishments. In most cases, their main success was in planting and maintaining churches for their own expatriate countrymen, rather than reaching out to indigenous populations with the gospel. On the rare occasions when such cross-cultural outreaches were initiated, the missionaries often faced resistance from their own colonial officials. European administrators in colonial cities were wary of any activity that could disrupt relations with the local population, and so the introduction of Christianity on a large scale—which would necessarily challenge the influence of local religions and thus stir up social resentment—was frowned upon.[26] Over the course of the eighteenth century, it gradually became clear that if Protestants were going to maintain a global mission effort, it would likely have to be organized on their own, not as a function of national colonization programs.

There was, however, one major exception to the patterns described above—a group of Protestants that was an outlier to the colonial program, and whose early success became an inspiration that paved the way for the explosion of missions at the end of the eighteenth century. These were the Moravians, an intrepid band of religious refugees who came under the protection of Count Zinzendorf of Germany. The

---

25 Walker, *History of the Christian Church*, 471; cf. Beeching, *Open Path*, 86.

26 See Porter, *Religion versus Empire*, 23; Etherington, *Missions and Empire*, 43; Marshall, *Making and Unmaking*, 44; Neill, *Colonialism and Christian Missions*, 14.

Moravians represented an outgrowth of continental Pietism, which by the turn of the eighteenth century had proven to be a profoundly missional movement and one which exercised significant influence on English Nonconformism.[27]

The Moravians of the early eighteenth century were not so much a denomination as a single community. The Moravian movement arose from a group of central European refugees, Protestants descended from the theological heritage of the Czech reformer Jan Hus. These Moravians, persecuted in their own homeland, were invited in 1722 to settle on the estate of a German nobleman, Count Nicolaus Ludwig von Zinzendorf, who shared many pietistic sentiments with the refugees.[28] They built a village called Herrnhut on Zinzendorf's lands, and Zinzendorf himself became a leader of their movement, which was marked by an emotionality uncommon in public Christianity. Such appeals to emotion were looked down upon as "enthusiasm" by many Protestant denominations, but some English Nonconformists saw an affinity with the Moravians in their own churches' growing embrace of emotionally affective rhetoric.

Just ten years after the settlement of Herrnhut, the Moravians sent out their first cross-cultural missionaries, aiming to introduce the gospel to the indigenous people of Greenland and to the enslaved populations in the British West Indies.[29] Along the way, they had several interactions with English Protestants, including a shipboard experience with John Wesley that changed the latter's life and propelled him toward his great endeavors in evangelism.

The example of the Moravians was powerful, but it does not quite merit being viewed as a similar explosive launch-point for global mission as the Nonconformist mission agencies of the 1790s. The Moravian mission movement was limited by its small size and cultural and linguistic context. Since it was the product of a small community,

---

27 Bosch, *Transforming Mission*, 260.

28 Tucker, *From Jerusalem*, 68–70.

29 Neill, *History of Christian Missions*, 236–38.

it was remarkable for what it achieved, but had limited influence on the broader scope of Protestant world missions (aside from a few areas of notable localized impact). It could not marshal the efforts of many hundreds or thousands of churches in concerted action, as other Protestant groups would later be able to do. Nonetheless, the Moravians' example was profoundly inspirational and served as one of many puzzling factors motivating English Christians to launch their own mission movement.[30] But even in saying that, it should be acknowledged that the legacy of Moravian missions was not one that was universally admired in the eighteenth century.

Many Nonconformists were suspicious of Moravian theology, believing that their emotionally saturated emphasis on the suffering of Christ was just a bit out of balance. Unlike most Protestant traditions, where Christ's sufferings were matched with a sense of individual guilt and sorrow over one's sins, Moravian theology and hymnody paired graphic descriptions of Christ's wounds with expressions of desire and delight.[31] The distaste evoked by this trend in Moravian theology contributed to John Wesley's later disavowal of his support for them, despite being inspired by their example as a young man. Wesley's hesitancy about Moravian associations likely delayed the development of a Methodist missionary enterprise longer than it would have otherwise taken, allowing the Nonconformists to become the first movers in that area instead.[32]

Aside from the Moravian mission movement, a few individual efforts were undertaken on the margins of European colonial claims. This occurred in the North American colonies, where the heirs of English Puritans lived in close proximity to indigenous non-Christian cultures. A few enterprising individuals took it upon themselves to evangelize the local Native Americans, including John Eliot in the

30 See Carey, *Enquiry*, 37.

31 See Marshall and Todd, *English Congregational Hymns*, 22–23.

32 See Mack, "Religious Dissenters," 1; Stanley, *History of the Baptist Missionary Society*, 2.

seventeenth century and David Brainerd in the eighteenth. As a young man, Brainerd traveled among Native American tribes in the northern and central American colonies, seeking to introduce them to Christianity. Particularly important in raising awareness of cross-cultural mission was the publication of Brainerd's journals, presented by Jonathan Edwards, a central figure of the Great Awakening. Edwards was himself involved in local outreach to Native Americans and wrote hopefully of a coming global revival.[33]

The work of Brainerd, as communicated by Edwards, had a formative influence on missiological thought in both American and English Protestant circles.[34] The hymnographer Philip Doddridge (of whom we will hear more in chapter 6) was at the forefront of introducing that work to England, serving as an editor of the British publication of Brainerd's journals.[35] Among all the ethnic groups with which Britain had contact in the eighteenth century, Native Americans loomed the largest in terms of the interest they sparked, and the accounts of their Christianization became part of the impetus for missional thinking for Doddridge and many others.[36] The small successes in the labors of Eliot, Brainerd, and others so encouraged the colonial churches that further attempts at organized missions were made. The Puritans of Massachusetts Bay Colony organized a society for propagating the gospel among the Native Americans, and various villages of so-called "praying Indians" were established.[37]

One can see in these efforts the germ of the later, large-scale movements for global evangelization that would eventually develop in the Anglophone churches, but their immediate results were limited. The devastating effects of European diseases on Native American populations, coupled with frequent warfare along colonial frontiers

---

33 Hutchinson, *Errand to the World*, 40–41; Olson, *Story of Christian Theology*, 503–4.

34 Klauber and Manetsch, *Great Commission*, 47.

35 See Doddridge, *Abridgement*.

36 Bickham, *Savages Within the Empire*, 3.

37 Tucker, *From Jerusalem*, 87.

and the hatreds that developed from those conflicts, all hindered the development of a sustainable, long-lasting mission to the Native Americans.

Further, it should be noted that geographical proximity was one of the defining factors in the motivation for such missions. The missionaries who went out were mainly just walking into the woods adjoining their own backyards. There was not a corresponding impetus to send out missionaries across the globe to distant nations. These were missions conducted on the margins of one's own home area, not an ambitious program of world evangelization. So while these colonial missions to Native Americans were established earlier than the great Protestant mission movement of the late eighteenth century, they did not yet reflect the large-scale vision that would come to characterize the global missionary enterprise. There was still something missing, but its influence was already percolating in the background: before Brainerd, before the Moravians, and before the revivals of the Great Awakening, the hymns of Isaac Watts were already making their rounds from church to church across England and America.

The Protestant Mission Movement

One of the key historical events this book focuses on is the launch of the Protestant mission movement, the great eruption in coordinated efforts to send missionaries across cultural, political, and linguistic boundaries to introduce the Christian faith to people groups who had no prior exposure to it. This movement spans from 1792 until at least the end of the nineteenth century (though some scholars trace its wave of activity up to the Edinburgh Missionary Conference of 1910, which subsequently produced further waves throughout the twentieth century). Popular and scholarly literature refers to this movement with many different terms, including the "Golden Age of Protestant Missions" and the "Great Century of Protestant Mission."[38]

38 See Norton, "Student Foreign Missions Fellowship," 17; Beeching, *Open Path*, 204; Tucker, *From Jerusalem*, 109–10.

While all of the available terms falter at one point or another, each one attempts to recognize a startling historical reality: that in the form, scope, and theological vision of the Protestant missionary wave of the late eighteenth century and throughout the nineteenth, something remarkably new had emerged in the history of Christianity.

The notable features of the Protestant mission movement can be considered in the three categories mentioned above—form, scope, and theological vision. In its form, the Protestant mission movement saw the establishment of independent societies for the organization and operation of missions. This was not an entirely new idea, but it was implemented with striking effect beginning in 1792, when William Carey laid out a vision for such societies in his missiological treatise, *An Enquiry into the Obligations of Christians to Use Means for the Conversion of the Heathens*. It was quickly given institutional form when, later that same year, twelve of Carey's ministerial colleagues founded the Baptist Missionary Society. This was followed in quick succession by the 1795 founding of the London Missionary Society, which, while largely led by Congregationalists, was explicitly inter-denominational in its organization.[39] (At this point, it is worth noting which groups stand at the forefront of the new mission movement: Baptists and Congregationalists, the same two wings of English Nonconformism that stood at the center of the earlier revolution in hymnody, of which we will have more to say in the next chapter.)

These mission societies represented a new outgrowth of the missionary enterprise, one that would eventually blossom into the many mission agencies and non-governmental aid organizations of the nineteenth and twentieth centuries. Most previous attempts at mission were centralized under the authority of existing institutions, such as a European monarchy, a colonial or commercial enterprise, or a church hierarchy. The new model of mission societies, arising from the dynamism of the free church tradition, allowed the mission to oversee

39 Neill, *History of Christian Missions*, 262; Goodall, *History of the London Missionary Society*, 2; Klauber and Manetsch, *Great Commission*, 54.

itself rather than being overseen by other authorities whose values and priorities did not match those of the missionaries. It also encouraged the participation of a wide range of Christians across a diverse array of denominations, allowing individual Christian laypeople and even whole congregations to participate in global missions by giving, praying, and sending out workers. Eventually, it would also enable the specialization of societies, allowing mission groups to become experts and leaders in areas like linguistics, community development, and medical aid.[40]

The Protestant mission movement also represents a sharp break from previous developments when one considers its scope. As mentioned above, most previous missions were conducted within colonial territories. There were occasional attempts to reach the indigenous people groups on the borders of those territories, but these seldom went beyond a limited mission on the margins.[41] No previous missionary ventures seriously contemplated sending missionaries ranging out beyond the established bounds of colonial territories. Beginning in the 1790s, however, that dynamic changed. Throughout the nineteenth century, it would be Protestant missionaries who were often the agents of first contact with indigenous cultures, whereas earlier it had been colonial officers or commercial officials. Missionaries like David Livingstone and J. Hudson Taylor would seek to reach people groups well beyond where their colonial representatives thought that it was safe to go. With the launch of the Protestant mission movement, suddenly the entire world lay open for Christian engagement, even areas far beyond the reach of traditional Christian governments.

The Protestant mission movement was also notable for its theological vision, which is one of the primary concerns of this book. Beginning with William Carey and some of his contemporaries, we suddenly have a clear articulation of a point that was not often made throughout the history of Christianity: that followers of Jesus have

40 See Latourette, *History of Christianity*, 1032–33; cf. Tilly, *Popular Contention*, 5–8.

41 See Irvin and Sunquist, *History of the World Christian Movement*, 326.

a mandate to spread the gospel of Christ's kingdom to every people, language, tribe, and nation on earth.[42] Earlier interpretive trends on the Great Commission had obscured this realization, as had some of the theological and ecclesiastical challenges described earlier in this chapter. While there were great exemplars of mission from every age of church history that one could look to for inspiration and instruction, the theological vision of the Protestant mission movement was striking for its clarity and its resounding call to action, presented as the obligation of every Christian and every denomination.

Looking for Clues

All of this prompts a question: If the Protestant mission movement of the 1790s represented such a significant new development, what were the factors that led to its rise? Even if prior missionary efforts could not match its explosive new dimensions, it remains true that most movements do not simply appear out of nowhere. The groundwork for such epoch-making historical shifts is usually laid quietly in the background over the course of decades.

In the case of the Protestant mission movement, some answers to that question are already well-known, and this book has touched on a few of them. Histories of mission give a great deal of credit to figures like William Carey, whose writings, organizational efforts, and missionary activities were the decisive flashpoint for the emergence of the movement in the 1790s.[43] In some cases, historians' emphasis on Carey's role (and a few of his contemporaries) tended to be overblown, making it sound like the entire movement was the product of his genius. Modern historiography casts doubt on narratives that attribute major transformations in history solely to a particular leader or hero; in most cases, the leader in question represents lines of thought that have been

42 See Wright, "Great Commission," 153–54; Akin, Merkle, and Robinson, *40 Questions*, 23–27.

43 See Tucker, *From Jerusalem*, 108, 113; cf. Stanley, *History of the Baptist Missionary Society*, 3.

percolating under the surface of society for some time. Still, Carey's contribution should not be underestimated, and his work provides an important framework for understanding the theological vision of the new movement.

Beyond the missiological genius of William Carey and his contemporaries, many historians point to the Evangelical Revival of the 1730s and '40s as the seedbed for the mission movement.[44] This revival—which was a trans-Atlantic movement, known in its North American version as the Great Awakening—introduced radical transformations into much of the English-speaking Christian world. Driven by the preaching ministries of such luminaries as John Wesley, George Whitefield, and Jonathan Edwards, the revival infused a new zeal for evangelism into English and American churches. Preachers addressed vast crowds in fields and city squares, often sparking fervent emotional responses. This event was a crucial turning point in the birth of what would come to be known as the evangelical movement, with its insistence on a cross-centered gospel, the centrality of Scripture, the necessity of a conversion experience, and the mandate for evangelistic witness.[45]

While the factors above certainly represent some developments that laid the groundwork for the Protestant mission movement, none alone tells the whole story. In the case of the Evangelical Revival, for instance, the groups most affected by it in England were not the Nonconformists who launched the first wave of the mission movement, but Anglicans and their offshoots. The major figures on the English side of the revival were all Anglicans—the Wesley brothers and George Whitefield—and the first major movement to emerge from it was one that would become altogether separate, the Methodists. English Nonconformists were often wary of the theological differences that accompanied their divisions from Anglicans and Methodists. They were also cautious of the emotionalism attached to the revival, fearing

44 See Klauber and Manetsch, *Great Commission*, 46; Routley, *English Religious Dissent*, 162.

45 Bebbington, *Evangelicalism in Modern Britain*, 2–3.

the pervasive effects of "enthusiasm" (a term that bore a negative connotation in the eighteenth century, suggesting emotions running wild to the detriment of reason and order). Wesley and Whitefield were looked down upon for their evangelistic tactics and their perceived embrace of "enthusiasm," and only the rare Nonconformist minister (like Philip Doddridge) would occasionally reach out to affirm and partner with their work, and then only in a limited way.[46]

Due to these hesitancies and the continuing influences of an ecclesiology focused on the local congregation, there was no direct link between the revivals and the Nonconformist mission movement, at least not a link by which the former could fully explain the latter. Even where one might expect to find connections between the revivals and global mission—as in John Wesley's connections to the Moravians—those expectations do not pan out. By the end of the eighteenth century, a widening gulf had developed between Wesley's Methodists and the Moravians, such that the latter's passion for world mission did not immediately transfer to the former.[47]

For as much as the revival did bring a fresh wind of excitement and zeal into English-speaking churches, it did not play out as straightforwardly as one might expect. It took nearly a century of cross-pollination for the effects of the Evangelical Revival to work their way across all the denominations that would eventually become "evangelical," and in the meantime, the global Protestant mission movement was launched by a wing of English church life that was less influenced by the revival than others.

Was there something else—some other element working among English Congregationalists and Baptists in the eighteenth century, preparing their hearts for mission? Indeed there was: a new form of congregational worship, which served as a powerful and unexpected source for infusing missional thinking into the life

46 Bailey, *Gospel in Hymns*, 66–67; Crawford, "Origins," 373; Benson, *English Hymn*, 258; see also Yeager, *Early Evangelicalism*, 5.

47 See Stanley, *History of the Baptist Missionary Society*, 2.

of English Christians. At the beginning of the century, the English Nonconformists were no more missional in their thinking than any other contemporary group (and by some measures, dramatically less so), yet a new wave of hymnody was about to bring missions back to the forefront of their imaginations, in a form that could be repeated, celebrated, and internalized whenever they gathered to worship.

3

The Songs of Zion in a Strange Land

How English Hymns Came to Be

We now have a sense of the main characters of this story—the Congregationalist and Baptist wings of English Nonconformism. It was the Baptists and Congregationalists who launched the first societies of the Protestant mission movement (in 1792 and 1795, respectively), and it was these two groups that stood at the vanguard of the earlier movement in hymnography. The new worship movement first started bearing fruit among the Baptists in the 1690s and then went on to dominate the worship of many different churches through the work of Congregationalist hymnographers in the early 1700s. To get a sense for the power of hymnody in this period, however, it is worthwhile to go back and remind ourselves of what congregational worship looked like for Nonconformists before the Golden Age of Hymns broke upon them.

For Baptists and Congregationalists, the two Nonconformist denominations at the heart of the change, worship was always centered on the preaching of the Bible. The two main ordinances of Christ—baptism and communion—retained their places of honor, though communion was generally practiced less frequently in this period of church history (across many denominations) than in some others. Nonconformists were particularly wary of placing too much emphasis on communion, largely as a reaction against the perceived

Catholic over-emphasis on the rite. As heirs of the Puritan-minded branch of the English Reformation, the Nonconformists held a suspicion of sacramental theology as being rather too superstitious for a biblically based faith. As such, the worship of their churches had shifted from the altar to the pulpit. Scripture alone was the guiding principle, and now in an even stronger sense than Martin Luther had imagined: "only in the eighteenth century did the Protestant watchword *sola Scriptura*, or 'the Bible alone,' begin to mean 'no authority except the Bible' instead of 'no authority over the Bible.'"[1]

The service of worship was focused on Scripture, which included any singing that was done. If song was present in the service, it was the biblical psalms that were sung. The choice to highlight biblical texts in song was driven by noble aims, of course: honoring inspired Scripture, whereas any alternative would be a mere human composition, subject to error. There was a nagging problem with an exclusive focus on psalmody, though, a problem that made the shift from psalms to hymns inevitable: If the church only sings psalms, then it can never sing directly about Jesus or the gospel message. While hints of Jesus abound in the psalms, limiting one's singing to them means restricting oneself to Scriptures that were a thousand years removed from the coming of the Messiah.

This preference for psalmody wasn't universal. The Reformation in German-speaking Europe included newly composed hymns from the very beginning, and a tradition of hymn-writing went back centuries further in both the Catholic and Orthodox worlds.[2] So why did English Christianity end up restricting itself to psalmody? The answer goes back to the peculiar way that the Reformation played out in Britain.

1 Noll, Komline, and Kantzer Komline, *Turning Points*, 214, 219–20.

2 See Bailey, *Gospel in Hymns*, 5; Templeton and Riglan, *Reforming Worship*, 78; Sherman, "Catechetical Function," 81.

Psalms and Hymns: The Reformation Heritage

Hymnody was a slowly developing field in England from the time of the English Reformation until the beginning of the eighteenth century. Prior to England's schism from Rome, hymnody had been a field dominated by the established liturgy of the Roman Catholic Church, which featured canticles and psalms, as well as a long tradition of Latin hymns. Many of those old Latin hymns dated back to the patristic period, to figures like Ambrose and Prudentius.[3]

This tradition of Latin hymnody, however, was not expressed in congregational singing; singing was done by priests or choristers.[4] As the Middle Ages wore on, Latin ceased to be the first language of most Catholics, and yet the liturgy and the hymns remained in Latin. Vernacular-language songs were generally not used in church services, and in the period immediately preceding the Reformation, the composition of new liturgical hymns had become uncommon.[5] That's not to say that there weren't any new songs being written on religious themes. There were many, as a glance at the canticles of Hildegard of Bingen and Francis of Assisi can attest. But such songs were not really written as hymns; they were not intended for widespread use in congregational singing. Medieval songs of devotion were used in personal and popular settings, but not in the public worship of the church.[6]

When the earliest movements of the Reformation began to arise, that picture changed. The Hussites of Bohemia anticipated the Protestant Reformation in many respects, not least of which was their embrace of congregational singing a century before similar practices emerged in Lutheran and Reformed congregations.[7]

---

3 Rorem, *Singing Church History*, 17–25.

4 Temperley, "All Skillful Praises," 531.

5 Gillman, *Evolution of the English Hymn*, 128.

6 Foote, *Three Centuries*, 5–6.

7 Gillman, *Evolution of the English Hymn*, 130; Benson, *English Hymn*, 20–21.

Martin Luther, leading the German Reformation, was also keen to harness the power of music to revitalize worship in languishing congregations. He famously adapted popular tunes and set them to new lyrics, specifically developed for use in church services (his hymn "A Mighty Fortress Is Our God" is the most well-known example). He also added a theological imperative to hymnody through his insistence on the priesthood of all believers, encouraging the entire congregation to participate in the work of singing. While it was still common for churches to have choirs to perform the songs of public worship, it gradually became more normal for churches to incorporate the congregation in songs as well.[8]

The Lutheran tradition thus launched its revolution in hymnody well in advance of the English-speaking world. It is worth noting, perhaps, that the Danish Lutherans were also earlier movers in Protestant world missions than most English churches, so the connection between hymns and missions might also be visible there. However, since it was the English mission movement, and not the German one, that threw open the floodgates of Protestant world missions in a startlingly new way at the end of the eighteenth century, we will keep our attention on English hymnody.

Why did English Protestantism not follow Luther's example and immediately launch a new form of hymnody? After all, the English Reformation was fundamentally a liturgical revolution, centered around a prayer-and-service book that left Latin behind and harnessed the vernacular language to speak directly to the hearts and minds of the people. If one were writing new prayers and adapting old ones into the vernacular, it would be just a small step further to take the old hymnographic traditions and set them loose in the English tongue.

That's not what happened, though. The recapturing of vernacular song in the Anglican church remained limited to a few traditional liturgical pieces and biblical canticles.[9] Although the Reformation

8 See Sykes, *Church and State*, 240–41.

9 Benson, *English Hymn*, 42–43; Bailey, *Gospel in Hymns*, 5.

was exercising its influence on English Christianity, Luther's version of the Reformation was not the only one, and in this case it was the other major stream—John Calvin's Reformed churches—that had a greater influence on early English worship. Calvinistic influences were strong in the Puritan wing of the Anglican church, as well as in many early Nonconformists—Particular Baptists, Presbyterians, and Congregationalists—and Calvin's Reformed tradition emphasized the use of biblical psalms rather than the composition of new hymns.[10]

There was a short-lived attempt, very early in the English Reformation, to introduce congregational hymnody along Lutheran lines (this can be seen, for instance, in Miles Coverdale's 1530 hymnal, *Ghoostly Psalmes and Spirituall Songes*), but the Reformed perspective, which viewed psalms as the most appropriate form of worship for the people of God, quickly won the day.[11] From the Reformed wing of the Reformation came books of psalms for public worship, rendered into metrical form for easy singing. Such metrical psalters convey the content of the biblical psalms according to a set rhyme-and-meter scheme, so that they can be sung to any number of standard melodies.

As an example of metrical psalmody, consider the opening lines of Psalm 23: "The Lord is my shepherd; I shall not want. He maketh me to lie down in green pastures: he leadeth me beside the still waters" (KJV). A famous metrical psalter, the 1650 book produced for the Scottish church, renders the same lines thus:

> The Lord's my shepherd, I'll not want.
> He makes me down to lie
>
> In pastures green: he leadeth me
> The quiet waters by.[12]

10 Benson, *English Hymn*, 22–23; Marshall and Todd, *English Congregational Hymns*, 12; Beynon, *Isaac Watts: Reason*, 144.

11 Gillman, *Evolution of the English Hymn*, 141–45; Foote, *Three Centuries*, 9–10.

12 *Scottish Metrical Psalter*, 34.

By setting the content of biblical psalms into a singable form, psalters enabled congregations to use the sung worship of ancient Israel as their own. While liturgical pieces and biblical canticles remained in use by priests and choristers, congregational song, when practiced, became largely a matter of psalmody and left no room for newly composed hymns.

Many modern readers, more familiar with hymns and worship songs, might look back at the days of psalmody with a sense of attraction: Wouldn't it be grand, after all, to just sing Scripture itself? No doubt that is true, and psalmody deserves a comeback in modern church life, but the mistake of the English churches was to insist on it as an *exclusive* form of worship. Psalmody appeared early in the English Reformation, first in family use and then in churches, and it held sway for nearly two hundred years.

Shortly after the French Reformed churches began creating metrical psalms in the 1530s, English versions also appeared. Thomas Sternhold and John Hopkins produced one of the first major English psalters in the mid-1500s. At first, the Sternhold-Hopkins psalter was used in domestic settings rather than in congregational worship. It was composed for families to have biblical songs to sing at home instead of popular ballads, and it was hoped to encourage the practice of communal family devotions.[13] The early years of the English Reformation saw the worship liturgy of the Church of England in a constant state of flux, swinging like a pendulum between Reformed and Catholic practices, creating an environment that was not conducive for any new form of worship to gain a consistent foothold. Congregational singing itself still felt like a rather revolutionary idea at this point. The question of whether psalms were preferable to hymns was still a long way off, and even the corporate singing of psalmody remained uncertain.

13 Temperley, "All Skillful Praises," 531–32.

The Sternhold-Hopkins psalter quickly became popular among Puritan families in the Anglican church, offering a simple, biblically based form of worship. This became essential to their practice during the persecutions under the Catholic Queen Mary in the 1550s. In homes and, whenever possible, in churches, the psalter enabled these Puritans to conduct services of Reformed worship without having to revert to the old Catholic missal.[14] Once Mary's reign had ended and her Protestant sister Elizabeth took the throne, the church of the English Reformation was ready to come back out of the shadows, now with the biblical psalms ringing from their lips.

The Sternhold-Hopkins psalter was reissued in 1562 in a final and definitive form, together with other major reforms in Anglican worship, and it quickly became a staple of Anglican practice. Along with the *Book of Common Prayer*, the Thirty-nine Articles, and the *Books of Homilies*, the psalter was now a core document of the English Reformation.[15] Because of its association with the Reformed wing of Protestant practice, the psalter also became a common feature in the worship of many Presbyterian, Particular Baptist, and independent Puritan congregations.

Despite the growing usage of the metrical psalter, there were several problems with using only the psalms in the church's sung worship. First, as already noted, it severely limited the content of what could be sung. Even accounting for prophetic foreshadowings in the text, there would still be no clear references to Jesus, the gospel, or the Christian life in congregational songs. Second, the role of psalms in Christian liturgy was somewhat limited. While there are songs of praise, thanksgiving, and lament, if one were looking for pieces to pair with specific movements of Christian liturgical rites, such as communion or baptism, one would look in vain. This consideration—the desire to have songs that fit the celebration of the Christian

14 Bailey, *Gospel in Hymns*, 11–14; Reynolds and Price, *Survey of Christian Hymnody*, 39–40.

15 Foote, *Three Centuries*, 26.

ordinances—drove early hymnographers to experiment with new compositions. The Baptists, in particular, wanted songs they could sing at baptism services, and these began appearing as early as the 1690s. There was also a slow but gradual acceptance of using hymns devoted to the celebration of the Lord's Supper by the end of the seventeenth century.[16] This followed the pattern of Christ and the disciples, who sang a hymn after sharing the first communion (Mark 14:26).

A third problem with the exclusive use of psalmody was that the psalms did not fit well with the musical culture of Europe at the time, making them an awkward addition to a service of Christian worship. When translated into a metrical version, a psalm could easily run into an absurd number of stanzas (often more than twelve), forcing congregations to either commit to a very long period of singing or reduce the number of verses by deciding which pieces of inspired Scripture were less fit for use than others.[17]

The length of the psalms was exacerbated by the method of singing commonly used at the time, called "lining out." Because most churches did not have the resources to provide enough physical books for everyone to have their own copy of the psalter, the singing had to proceed line by line. The song leader would sing the first line, and the congregation would sing it back. Then the song leader would sing the second line, and the congregation would sing it back, and so on, effectively doubling the length of an already long song.[18]

Furthermore, as the New Testament continued to be studied during the Protestant Reformation, it became clear that an exclusive focus on the psalms was not the early Christian pattern. While the psalms were used for worship in the New Testament period, evidence from the New Testament indicates that the first Christians were also composing new songs of their own (see Eph 5:19; Col 3:16), some of which might even appear in the pages of Scripture (for example,

---

16 Lamport, et al., *Hymns and Hymnody*, 165; Wykes, "From David's Psalms," 234.

17 See Beynon, *Isaac Watts: Reason*, 145.

18 Marshall and Todd, *English Congregational Hymns*, 18.

Phil 2:6–11). Even the biblical psalms themselves supported the practice, with the oft-repeated command to "Sing unto the Lord a new song" (Pss 96:1; 98:1; 149:1; see also 33:3; 40:3; 144:9). Given that the biblical model in both the Old and New Testaments allowed for the composition of new songs, it was natural that Christians would eventually expand the field of congregational singing with compositions that expressed their own voice in worship.

Psalms and Hymns in the Sixteenth and Seventeenth Centuries

It took more than a century and a half from the first stirrings of the English Reformation for new hymns to become an accepted vehicle for worship. There were early attempts at writing hymns, but they were not usually intended for congregational use. Throughout the sixteenth and early seventeenth centuries, various poets published collections of "hymns" (as, for instance, those by John Donne, George Herbert, and John Milton)—but these were devotional poems, as this was what the term "hymn" generally referred to at the time, not compositions intended for congregational singing.[19] In some circles, even well into the eighteenth century, hymn texts were still largely used for reading in private devotional settings rather than for public singing.[20]

The difficulties with singing psalms in worship quickly became apparent with the widespread adoption of psalmody. To add to the theological and practical difficulties of an exclusive focus on the psalms, the Sternhold-Hopkins psalter faced repeated criticism for both translation and style.[21] This led to the production of other metrical psalters, including the Ainsworth Psalter (1612) and the Ravenscroft Psalter (1620). The former was used by Separatists, some of whom carried it to North America as the settlers of Plymouth

19 Benson, *English Hymn*, 63–65; Reynolds and Price, *Survey of Christian Hymnody*, 50; Knapp, "Isaac Watts," 465.

20 Phillips, "Cotton Mather," 205.

21 Davies, *Worship and Theology*, 65.

Colony. Another new psalter soon appeared in the neighboring colony when the leaders of Massachusetts created the Bay Psalm Book (1640), notable both as the first book published in the English colonies of North America and for its long and profound effect on Christian worship in those colonies.[22] Still another psalter from the mid-seventeenth century had enormous impact on the broader English-speaking world: the Scottish Metrical Psalter (1650), which found a wide reception in Presbyterian circles, since it was the official psalter-translation approved by the Presbyterian Church of Scotland.

Each of these psalters, however, failed to meet the dual expectations of beauty and textual fidelity. In the words of Louis Benson, a historian of hymnody, "The men who made their Psalters were not poets nor even good craftsmen."[23] It was only at the end of the seventeenth century that a new psalter appeared which began to gain some acceptance as a standard replacement for the Sternhold-Hopkins "Old Version." This was the *New Version of the Psalms of David* (or "New Psalter") by Nahum Tate and Nicholas Brady (1696), which added a more refined poetic sensibility to the text. Still, Sternhold-Hopkins persisted in many churches well into the eighteenth century, and its surviving editions outnumbered those of the Tate-Brady version in every decade until the 1790s.[24] The Old Psalter's widespread use was not necessarily a mark of its popularity; it continued to evoke public bemoaning of its "miserable, scandalous doggerel."[25] By the end of the century, writes M. Pauline Parker, "both [psalters] came to be despised."[26]

22 Lamport, et al., *Hymns and Hymnody*, 151–54; Foote, *Three Centuries*, 3; cf. Stevenson, "Watts in America," 206.

23 Benson, *English Hymn*, 46.

24 Marshall and Todd, *English Congregational Hymns*, 16–19; Temperley, "All Skillful Praises," 553.

25 John Wesley, quoted in Phillips, *Hymnody Past and Present*, 171.

26 Parker, "Hymn as a Literary Form," 406.

There were some minor attempts in the seventeenth century to write hymns for worship beyond the corpus of biblical psalms, though none found widespread acceptance until after Watts's "improvement of psalmody" (to use his own term). Walking the line between psalms and hymns was William Barton, a Puritan cleric who produced his own translation of the psalter and later, near the end of his life, published several hundred hymns based on careful translations of other passages of Scripture. They were hymns in the sense that they were intended for singing, but perhaps not in the sense of being free artistic creations.[27] One of the more prominent hymnographers of this early period was Thomas Ken, an Anglican bishop, but his contributions were only put to congregational use much later. Of all the seventeenth-century religious poets whose works would come to be used in hymnody, it was only Ken, says historian Frederick Gillman, "who understood how to write a good hymn."[28] Among Ken's works is "Praise God from Whom All Blessings Flow" (aka "the Doxology"), which likely constitutes the most often-sung lines in all of English hymnody:

> Praise God from whom all blessings flow;
> Praise him, all creatures here below;
> Praise him above, ye heavenly hosts;
> Praise Father, Son, and Holy Ghost.

Ken's hymnography was influential in later Anglican developments, but most of his hymns had little initial impact and were not even included in the first printed editions of his work.[29]

Another representative of this early group was Samuel Crossman, who included a few metrical songs in a 1664 publication. They were not widely used as congregational hymns at the time, but some, like his "My Song Is Love Unknown," were later reintroduced and subsequently maintained their place in English hymnody. Other figures, like John

27 Benson, *English Hymn*, 60–62.

28 Gillman, *Evolution of the English Hymn*, 166.

29 Benson, *English Hymn*, 69–70.

Austin, also produced original hymns, though no one reached anything close to the breakthrough level of contemporary usage that Isaac Watts's works would achieve in the eighteenth century.[30]

Nahum Tate and Nicholas Brady also introduced some hymns of their own, including a few original songs in a supplement to their "New Version" psalter. This small collection saw limited use but helped set the precedent that hymns might be allowed in Anglican worship as a supplement to the psalms. Their songs included one that is still in common use, "While Shepherds Watched Their Flocks." This song falls within the long tradition of Christmas carols, which had been present in English society since the thirteenth century, but which were not generally considered hymns for the public worship of the church.[31]

The hymnographers mentioned above all represent developments within the Anglican stream of English hymnody, in which a handful of poetically inclined churchmen put forward hymns of their own creation but did not press for their introduction into weekly services of worship. In Nonconformist circles, the new form was developing more rapidly and finding immediate use, at least in a few congregations. Richard Baxter, a Puritan clergyman who became a reluctant dissenter in the 1660s, had written a few original hymns, but they saw only limited use.[32] John Mason, an Anglican, produced a book of hymns in 1683 that had only a small impact on Anglican worship, but which was popular enough among Nonconformists to run through eight editions by the time Watts began his work.[33] The Bible commentator Matthew Henry also produced his own volume of hymns, but he designated their use specifically for the home, not the church.[34]

30 Benson, 68–69.

31 Parker, "Hymn as a Literary Form," 398; Benson, *English Hymn*, 19, 80–81.

32 Lamport, et al., *Hymns and Hymnody*, 148; cf. Phillips, *Hymnal*, 92.

33 Benson, *English Hymn*, 71.

34 Williams, *Memoirs*, 110.

Early Baptists and the First Congregational Hymns

By the 1690s, a few Baptists were not only writing singable Christian poems but also putting them to use within their local congregations. One such figure was Benjamin Keach, a major representative of the Nonconformist contribution to creative literature.[35] Keach was the pastor of a Baptist church and one of the earliest figures to write hymns specifically for congregational singing. He based his argument for hymns on the proposition that they were interpretations of Scripture, just as sermons were.[36] Keach had roots in both major branches of the Baptist movement—he grew up under the influence of General Baptist theology but later converted to Calvinist beliefs (such as those held by Particular Baptists) in his early adulthood.

The General Baptists tended to favor a position that, like the Quakers, gave little room for congregational singing in church services. As the records of their assembly of 1689 state, "It was not considered anyways safe to admit such carnal formalities."[37] This position hearkened back to the attitude of one of the original Baptist founders, John Smyth, who preferred spontaneous worship over set forms like printed songs or written prayers.[38] Particular Baptists were more open to the use of song, but the printing of Keach's hymns in the 1690s sparked controversy within the denomination, leading to an acrimonious exchange of published pamphlets throughout most of that decade and resulting in a split within Keach's own congregation.[39] Despite their mixed initial reception, a few of Keach's hymns were so lovely that they later gained somewhat wider use, such as his "O Lord, 'Tis a Matter of High Praise" (selected stanzas shown):

---

35 See Wallace, *Shapers of English Calvinism*, 27.

36 Keach, *Banquetting House*, preface.

37 Davies, *Worship and Theology*, 126–27.

38 Gillman, *Evolution of the English Hymn*, 177–78.

39 Lamport, et al., *Hymns and Hymnody*, 134; Benson, *English Hymn*, 97–99; Rivers and Wykes, *Dissenting Praise*, 25; Wootton, "Wilderness and Christian Song," 82.

O Lord, 'tis matter of high praise,
Thy Word on us doth shine,
But happy they who feel its rays,
And glorious power divine.

We therefore throw our crowns below
Thy high and glorious throne;
And must all say, both night and day,
Thou worthy art alone,

All glory, power, and praise to have,
By us forevermore;
Thus let us sing unto our King,
And him in heart adore.[40]

Such early Nonconformist hymns were published and circulated, but they were not yet widely used in congregations outside each hymnographer's own church. Isaac Marlow, a vocal opponent of Benjamin Keach's hymn-writing work, noted in 1691 that he knew of only seven or eight out of a hundred Particular Baptist churches in England that were in favor of hymns, and only two that actually used hymns in worship.[41] The hymn-writing of the figures mentioned above (along with a few others) made some small impact, but, as Louis Benson notes, "Such use was exceptional; the books marking the tentative efforts of progressive individuals rather than the general practice."[42] Nevertheless, their use indicates a change in the ecclesiastical culture of Nonconformist churches, which were beginning to allow more room for creative endeavors in their worship.

From this background, it is clear that hymns were already gaining popularity by the time Isaac Watts came on the scene. The popularity of his hymns, however, would change the entire landscape of congregational song in Nonconformist churches (and most especially

40 Keach, *Spiritual Songs*, 55.

41 Rivers and Wykes, *Dissenting Praise*, 24.

42 Benson, *English Hymn*, 106.

in Congregationalist and Baptist churches). This is not, however, merely another story of a great man whose labors revolutionized the world; it is the story of how missional thinking influenced his hymns in the most surprising of ways, almost without him even realizing it.

Isaac Watts and the Transformation of Hymnody

The pivotal moment of change came with Isaac Watts's publication of major collections of original hymns, beginning in the first decade of the eighteenth century (of which more will be said in the next chapter). Instead of a small-scale program of hymns intended for localized use, they were now being disseminated in a form adapted for widespread use. The early endeavors of the late seventeenth century, however, had not completely smoothed the way; most Nonconformist denominations were still characterized by "violent antipathies against hymn-singing."[43] Nonetheless, after Watts's major works were published, sentiment shifted toward the use of hymns, especially among Congregationalists and Particular Baptists.

The changes brought about by the popularization of Watts's work were not mere happenstance. Watts was intentionally embarking on a program of writing and publication with the aim of effecting "an improvement of psalmody" in the life of the English church.[44] This program, which he called his "system of praise," was centered around one major aim: to allow Christian congregations to proclaim the praises of Christ through their singing. The limitation of using only psalmody, at least in Watts's eyes, was that psalters were based on a set of texts that predated the advent of Christ, and thus provided no opportunity for Christians to declare the truths of New Testament revelation in their songs.[45]

---

43 Stevenson, "Dr. Watts," 235.

44 Watts, *Hymns and Spiritual Songs*, 233.

45 Watts, *Psalms of David Imitated*, xvi–xviii; see Cousland, "Significance of Isaac Watts," 292.

The transition from psalm-singing to hymn-singing, largely brought about by Watts, was not smooth, but it was striking. In the words of one historian, "We might almost say that before Watts, English churches sang Psalms. After Watts, they sang hymns."[46] Watts's work was, to quote the hymnologist Frederick Gillman, "epoch-making… If he was not the first to set the form of the congregational hymn, he definitely established it as the normal medium of public praise."[47] By the time of his death in 1748, his hymns were being widely used throughout all the Nonconformist denominations (with the exception of Quakers).[48]

The new wave of hymns, though no longer restricted to the psalms, still drew heavily on biblical material. Many of the hymns were either paraphrases or expositions of biblical passages, but there was scope within the new form to explore beyond a direct rendition of biblical texts. Hymns could also serve as a poetic form of theological education, and Watts and his imitators made good use of this potential. Hymns began to expound upon Christology and Trinitarian theology, neither of which could be found in a traditional psalter. In reference to Isaac Watts's hymns, Madeleine Marshall and Janet Todd note that the hymnographer's purpose was "the controlled education of the religious sensibility of his singers."[49]

This "religious sensibility" was not only a matter of doctrine, though—it also had to do with the affective revolution evident in both continental Pietism and the Evangelical Revival of the 1730s. This trend was already in motion by Watts's time and placed more emphasis on emotionally evocative expressions of praise. The new hymns were part of a shift occurring in Nonconformist worship, moving from an objective viewpoint that focused on God's works to a more subjective viewpoint of the worshiper's response to God.[50] While individual faith

---

46 Herzel, *To Thee We Sing*, 142.

47 Gillman, *Evolution of the English Hymn*, 211.

48 Watts, *Dissenters*, 312.

49 Marshall and Todd, *English Congregational Hymns*, 56.

50 Davies, *Worship and Theology*, 99–100.

was often practiced with a great deal of emotionally affective piety in the sixteenth and seventeenth centuries (as can be seen in many writings of the Protestant Reformers and English Puritans), it was not until the eighteenth century that public displays of emotional piety began to be considered normal (and then only in a few circles).[51]

Prior to the eighteenth century, Nonconformist writing tended to prize a simple, clear, and unadorned style, but that tendency changed with the turn of the century.[52] Isaac Watts stood at the forefront of this revolution, regularly using language and phrasing that were more emotionally evocative than standard formulations. Watts felt that the "passions" (his preferred term for human emotions in worship) had an indispensable place in one's relationship with God. This emotive sensibility can be seen, for instance, in the opening lines of one of Watts's hymns:

> Awake, my heart, arise, my tongue,
> Prepare a tuneful voice,
> In God, the life of all my joys,
> Aloud I will rejoice.[53]

And in the preface to his *Hymns and Spiritual Songs*, Watts expressed how he intentionally infused the emotions of piety into his hymn texts:

> The most frequent tempers and changes of our spirit, and conditions of our life are here copied, and the breathings of our piety expressed according to the variety of our passions, our love, our fear, our hope, our desire, our sorrow, our wonder and our joy, as they are refined into devotion.[54]

Later in the eighteenth century, this trend would be expanded through John and Charles Wesley's intentional use of emotional

51 See Goodman, "Tears I Shed," 701.

52 See Keeble, *Literary Culture*, 246–50.

53 Watts, *Hymns and Spiritual Songs*, 2nd ed., 18.

54 Watts, iii.

appeals in their preaching and hymns. The Wesleys, also influenced by German Pietism, elevated the emotional expressiveness of English hymnody to a new level, one that matched the awakening fervor of the Evangelical Revival.[55] Other contemporary preachers—most of whom were not inclined to display emotion in preaching, such as Jonathan Edwards (who was known to read his sermons in a flat monotone)—nevertheless argued that the public expression of pious emotion was beneficial, and perhaps even a necessary element of a true Christian life. "If the great things of religion are rightly understood," Edwards wrote, "they will affect the heart."[56]

With such significant shifts in the content, psychology, and practice of hymnody now in view, we must turn our attention more fully to the character who stands at the center of that transition: the man known for his excellence in an astounding number of roles; pastor, theologian, hymnographer, poet, educator, and logician—Isaac Watts.

55 Marshall and Todd, *English Congregational Hymns*, 20–21.

56 Edwards, *Religious Affections*, 26.

4

Isaac Watts
The Logician Who Made the World Sing

Just as the churches at the center of this story are unlikely protagonists—English Nonconformists, only just emerging from the shadow of persecution—so the main figure in the story is also an unlikely character. Isaac Watts was an impressively gifted man in some respects, but an odd one in others. He was supremely talented in creating theologically rich and poetically lovely hymns—at a level that few have ever matched, either before or since. However, he was also a man whose boundless interests led him into forays into entirely different fields, like logic and educational theories, and whose chosen career as a minister never quite materialized in the ways he had hoped.

He was born into a family that had long experiences with the persecutions of the age. Suffering for one's faith was a way of life, and these familial trials gave Watts some of the toughness and resolve he would draw on during the hymn controversies of his adult life. His mother's side of the family came from French Huguenot stock—Protestant refugees from the fierce Catholic backlash on the continent. They had to flee their homes and take up a new life in England, where an expatriate Huguenot community blossomed in Spitalfields, the same east-London area that housed other religious outcasts, like the Baptists.[1]

1 Gillman, *Evolution of the English Hymn*, 211.

Isaac's father (also named Isaac Watts) served as a deacon of the Above Bar Congregational Church (so named because of its proximity to Bar Gate near the center of London). This church had formed from the followers of Rev. Nathaniel Robinson, a former Anglican priest who had refused to conform to the Act of Uniformity in 1662. In the quarter-century following that act, meeting together as a Nonconformist congregation was an illegal undertaking, for which the laity could be fined and the church leaders imprisoned. Such was the case with Isaac Watts's father, who served several prison sentences for his role in leading the Above Bar Congregational Church.[2]

Isaac Watts was born in 1674, during the height of the troubles for his church family. He was the oldest of eight children, and his father was absent from significant portions of his childhood because of the family's uncompromising stand for their beliefs. Watts noted in a journal that when he was nine years old, his father had been imprisoned for six months. Following that incident, a further separation of two years was necessary, as his father was forced to go into hiding apart from his family. Despite his absence, his father's example and instruction (by way of exhortatory letters) proved to be a shaping influence in young Isaac's life.[3]

The year 1688 was momentous for the Watts family. That was the year of the Glorious Revolution, in which the Protestant ruler William of Orange came over from the Netherlands to claim the English throne. The new king, a Dutch Calvinist, had deep-running Protestant sympathies that made him closer in doctrine and practice to many of the Nonconformists than to the Anglicans, despite the fact that he was now the legal head of the Anglican Church. One of the first moves of William's reign was to pass the Act of Toleration, which allowed Nonconformists the freedom to meet and worship as they pleased. The persecution and imprisonments that had formed such a major part of Isaac Watts's early family experiences were over.

2 Beynon, *Isaac Watts: His Life*, 12.

3 Bailey, *Gospel in Hymns*, 45; Beynon, *Isaac Watts: His Life*, 13; Fountain, *Isaac Watts Remembered*, 17–19.

Nonconformists would still be frowned upon and shut out of numerous social opportunities, but the era of active persecution was now largely a thing of the past.

1688 was also a momentous year for a much more personal reason: It was the year that Isaac, at the age of fourteen, underwent a transformative experience of conviction for his sins and of trusting in Christ for his salvation. Though the roots of his Christian faith were evident much earlier in his life than 1688, it was that year that he would later look back upon as the moment of his conversion.[4]

This sense of conviction for sin and the grace afforded by Christ would become an abiding theological theme for Isaac Watts, as for much Nonconformist thought and practice. In Watts's case, however, they were far more than simply a foundational piece of doctrine; they were truths that called forth emotionally laden responses, to be expressed in the medium to which he had naturally gravitated, even as a child: the composition of poetical verse. One early poem, written at six years old, displays many of the themes of Watts's later life, already nearly fully formed—his sense of his own sinfulness, the wonder of the grace of Christ, and a desire to sing praises as one's proper response. The poem was composed as an acrostic based on the letters of his name:

> **I** am a vile polluted lump of earth,
> **S**o I've continued ever since my birth;
> **A**lthough Jehovah grace does daily give me,
> **A**s sure this monster Satan will deceive me,
> **C**ome, therefore, Lord, from Satan's claws relieve me.
> **W**ash me in thy blood, O Christ,
> **A**nd grace divine impart,
> **T**hen search and try the corners of my heart,
> **T**hat I in all things may be fit to do
> **S**ervice to thee, and sing thy praises too.[5]

---

4 Bailey, 45; Beynon, 18.

5 Gibbons, *Memoirs*, 5.

Isaac Watts's education also strengthened his deep-rooted position in Nonconformism. His childhood education was typical for its day, but Watts was an uncommon student, showing an affinity for logic and excelling in languages. He became fluent in Latin, Greek, Hebrew, and French before the age of fourteen, and early biographers noted that he had begun his Latin studies far in advance of his contemporaries, at just four years of age.[6] This intellectual giftedness was evident throughout his life; later in his career, he would become well known not only as a hymnographer but also as an educational theorist, penning treatises on logic that were widely used in English schools. When the time came for Watts to leave grammar school at the age of sixteen, he faced an uncomfortable choice: either to follow the socially expected path and enroll at one of the two great universities in the land, Oxford or Cambridge, or to choose a path of less social promise by attending a dissenting academy.

While Nonconformist worship was now tolerated in England, Nonconformists still faced prejudices and barriers in their social lives and employment, and anyone seeking to enter public office would be expected and required to "conform" by participating in Anglican worship. The same was true for university students; conforming to Anglicanism was a requirement for anyone attending Oxford or Cambridge. Watts did not feel that he could do this, so he chose to enroll in a dissenting academy in Stoke Newington, just north of London. This choice would meet his immediate goals of furthering his education, but would also effectively seal his future against public office or civil service and cement him in Nonconformism for good. Dissenting academies did not present the same opportunities as a university education, but they were rigorous in their studies and had a wide influence in England.[7] Watts's alma mater had several distinguished alumni in his day, including the novelist Daniel Defoe, famous for Robinson Crusoe. It was run by Thomas Rowe, a tutor

6 See Jennings and Doddridge, *Works*, iv; Gibbons, *Memoirs*, 3.

7 Wilkinson, *1662—And After*, 104–5.

who exercised a considerable influence on Watts's thought, both in education and theology.[8]

After his studies at Stoke Newington were complete, Watts returned to his family home for about two years, and it was during this period—the mid-1690s—that Isaac Watts began to experiment with writing hymns. According to the traditional story, the impulse for this work came from a conversation with his father following a church service one Sunday. After they had returned home, young Isaac Watts complained about the songs they had to sing in church (which were based on metrical psalters and the stilted lines of William Barton), and his father responded by challenging him to write something better.[9] The younger Watts took up the challenge and composed his first hymn, "Behold the Glories of the Lamb," based on the heavenly scene of worship described in Revelation 5:9 (selected stanzas are shown here):

> Behold the glories of the Lamb
> Amidst his Father's throne:
> Prepare new honours for his name,
> And songs before unknown.
>
> Now to the Lamb that once was slain,
> Be endless blessings paid;
> Salvation, glory, joy remain
> Forever on thy head.
>
> Thou hast redeemed our souls with blood,
> Hast set the prisoners free,
> Hast made us kings and priests with God,
> And we shall reign with thee.[10]

This hymn would eventually be published a decade later as the opening work of his 1707 *Hymns and Spiritual Songs*. This first piece of Watts's

---

8 Armstrong, *Church of England*, 42; Stephenson, "Isaac Watts's Education," 364–65.

9 Gibbons, *Memoirs*, 254; cf. Beynon, *Isaac Watts: His Life*, 22.

10 Watts, *Hymns and Spiritual Songs*, 1–2.

hymnody, in addition to displaying his remarkable talent, underscores his conviction that Christians ought to be able to compose new hymns about Jesus to be used in worship, as the final lines of the first stanza emphasize: "Prepare new honours for his name, / And songs before unknown."

Isaac Watts's first employment came with his return to the academy town of Stoke Newington, where he became a chaplain and private tutor for the family of a Member of Parliament, Sir John Hartopp.[11] Hartopp was a Nonconformist, a position that had cost him nearly £7,000 in fines (it was now possible at this stage for Nonconformists to hold office, though with severe penalties, by making use of a temporary loophole called occasional conformity). The Hartopp family attended a Congregational church in Mark Lane, London, and Watts attended with them, occasionally being asked to preach. Within just a few years, by 1698, he had begun to serve as assistant to the church's pastor, and in 1702, after that pastor's departure, he consented to become the head pastor and was duly ordained into the Congregational ministry. Even at this early date, however, it was clear that Watts's health was frail and might jeopardize his ability to serve in the pastorate (as would prove to be the case later). Even as the church called him to ministry, congregational records indicate that because of Watts's bodily weakness, they were not necessarily expecting him to continue long in the ministry.[12]

It was during this early period of pastoral ministry that Watts began his hymn writing in earnest. In his first year of ministry, he started to introduce his hymns in the worship service. On March 29, 1702, he had his congregation sing a hymn of his own composition after the celebration of the Lord's Supper, and it appears to have been favorably received.[13] His church grew and relocated to Bury Street, and he garnered increasing attention as a leader within Nonconformism.

11 Gibbons, *Memoirs*, 92–96; see also Jacob, *Lay People*, 101.

12 Davis, *Isaac Watts*, 247.

13 Bond, *Poetic Wonder*, 40–41.

Watts began publishing both treatises and poetry, which led to the printing of a few hymns as part of his poetry book, *Horae Lyricae,* in 1706. His hymn-publishing career is usually considered to have started the following year, 1707, in large part because the hymnic portion of *Horae Lyricae* is experimental and not intended to be used as a hymnal (unlike his immediately following work, *Hymns and Spiritual Songs*). The poems of *Horae Lyricae* were an ambitious literary undertaking, and they earned Watts a mention in Dr. Samuel Johnson's classic book, *Lives of the Poets.*[14]

The first part of *Horae Lyricae* consists of original hymn texts, titled "Songs and Hymns Sacred to Devotion." This collection of thirty-nine hymns represents only a small portion of the hymns Watts had already begun working on, the remainder of which would appear in his hymnbook the following year. The hymnic portion of *Horae Lyricae* was designed as a sort of trial balloon for his hymn-writing projects, and it is clear from his introduction that he was not sure how they would be received.[15] He defends his work from attacks by secular scholars, arguing that hymn texts should not be judged by the same standards as literary poetry, as well as from attacks by his Christian audience, which was accustomed to a hymnic tradition dominated by the psalter alone. "These are but a small part of two hundred hymns of the same kind which are ready for public use," Watts writes, "if the world receive favourably what I now present." He then goes on to express his hesitancy, feeling that these hymns "differ too much from the usual methods of speech in which holy things are proposed to the general part of mankind."[16]

But the reception of *Horae Lyricae* must have been favorable enough, because Isaac Watt's landmark hymnbook, *Hymns and Spiritual Songs,* came out the next year and went on to change the shape of Christian hymnody. This book, the first major piece in Watts's program for the "improvement of psalmody," quickly succeeded in doing what no other

14 Johnson, *Lives of the English Poets,* 517; see also Phillips, *Hymnal,* 163.

15 Phillips, *Hymnal,* 88.

16 Watts, *Horae Lyricae,* n.p.

collection of English hymns had yet been able to do: establish regular usage in the weekly worship of many different congregations. Given the rate of editions produced, it is clear that Watts's hymnbook was popular. Although historical sources do not permit a direct tracing of congregational usage of Watts's hymnody, it appears that his hymns caught on even more quickly in the countryside than in his own circles in London, and eventually spread to the point of being nearly ubiquitous in Congregational worship by the end of his career.[17]

While widely used, it was a controversial book from the beginning, and Watts knew it would be. It went directly against the prevailing belief that the biblical psalms alone should suffice for the sung worship of the church. Even the title of his book was an implicit argument for the inclusion of songs beyond the psalms in Christian worship; it alludes to Ephesians 5:19, in which the apostle Paul enjoins Christians to use not psalms alone, but "psalms and hymns and spiritual songs" (KJV).

Yet the confidence of Watts's argument had grown considerably from his tentative and apologetic preface to *Horae Lyricae* a year before. In the opening sentence of *Hymns and Spiritual Songs*, he wrote that singing is the part of worship that brings one nearest to the experience of heaven, "and 'tis a pity that this of all others should be performed the worst upon earth."[18] He even dared to criticize certain aspects of psalmody, arguing that the biblical psalms too often fail to raise the Christian's heart in true devotion. He believed that some lines of the psalms were more suited to the dispensation of the Law than to the dispensation of grace in Christ. This was a challenge to a longstanding and venerable Protestant tradition, but Watts was no stranger to controversy. He did make some earnest concessions, however, accommodating the popular belief that only biblical texts should be used in worship by basing each of his hymns in the book's

17 Benson, *English Hymn*, 123–24; Gillman, *Evolution of the English Hymn*, 207; Gibbons, *Memoirs*, 306.

18 Watts, *Hymns and Spiritual Songs*, iii.

leading section on a verse or passage of Scripture. In the first edition of the book, he also appended "A Short Essay toward the Improvement of Psalmody," in which he presented a fuller treatment of his argument.

Hymns and Spiritual Songs, in its first edition, consisted of two hundred and ten hymns (plus additional doxologies at the end). The book was so successful, though, that it was quickly re-released in 1709 in an expanded version with three hundred sixty-five hymns and doxologies, ultimately going through sixteen editions during Watts's lifetime. The 1709 edition is now considered the standard form of the work.

Watts continued in ministry at the Bury Street church until 1712, at which point his frail constitution, which beset him with incapacitating bouts of illness, forced him to take an extended leave of about four years. With his assistant pastor, Samuel Price, taking over ministry duties for the church, Watts relocated to the country home of Sir Thomas Abney, a Nonconformist businessman, where he resumed his earlier role as a family tutor and household chaplain.

This mode of employment led him to compose his second book of hymns, *Divine Songs Attempted in Easy Language for the Use of Children,* which was published in 1715, along with a catechism for children that saw wide use throughout the eighteenth and nineteenth centuries. While this book was shorter than *Hymns and Spiritual Songs,* it also gained tremendous popularity and ran through seventeen editions during Watts's life. It eventually became a standard text in both churches and schools by the turn of the nineteenth century and is now regarded as one of the foundational works of children's literature.[19] Watts was an exceptional thinker and writer for many reasons, and his works for children give evidence for one more: he was among the first major English writers to write with a keen sense of children's sensibilities and levels of understanding.[20]

---

19 Phillips, *Hymnal,* 108, 117–21.

20 Rogal, "Watts' *Divine and Moral Songs,*" 100.

By 1716, Watts was able to resume some of his pastoral duties, but he continued to live with the Abneys for the rest of his life and benefited from their patronage. He published one more collection of hymns, *Psalms of David Imitated in the Language of the New Testament* (1719), which would prove to have a resounding impact on the worship and practice of Nonconformist churches. He had been working on his translation of the psalms for the better part of two decades, concurrently with his earlier projects, but wanted to publish *Hymns and Spiritual Songs* first to gauge public reaction and shield his *Psalms of David* from the initial waves of criticism.[21]

Psalms of David Imitated added new classics to the Christian repertoire, including "Jesus Shall Reign Where'er the Sun," "O God, Our Help in Ages Past," and "Joy to the World." In creating this hymnbook, Watts furthered his reformation of psalmody by rewriting the biblical psalms as Christian hymns. This was a far cry from producing just another metrical psalter, though. Watts was not content merely to put the psalm's words into appropriate rhyme and meter; he wanted to render the psalms as explicitly Christian songs, with references to Jesus and the teachings of the New Testament. Part of his motivation for doing this was his belief that psalm-singing often failed to engage the hearts of worshipers, for the same reasons he had outlined in his preface to *Hymns and Spiritual Songs*. In the opening pages of *Psalms of David Imitated,* he wrote that his purpose was "to introduce warm devotion into this part of divine worship."[22]

There were also secondary reasons for Watts's emendation of the biblical psalms. He felt that many of the psalms' expressions were more suited to articulating faith under the Old Covenant and lost some of their relevance when addressing the condition of Christians living under the New Covenant. And it was not just theological concerns that required a transposition from Old Covenant to New; Watts also

21 Bishop, *Isaac Watts*, xx.

22 Watts, *Psalms of David Imitated*, iv.

amended many of the psalms' verses on practical matters to make them more amenable to an eighteenth-century Protestant reading.[23]

Taking each of the psalms, he wrote them in hymn form, incorporating regular references to Jesus, the church, and the Christian life throughout. In many cases, Watts would write multiple hymns based on the same psalm, devoting several hymns to progressive portions of a psalm or producing differently metered versions of the same lines. Like its predecessors, this hymnbook became widely popular (though, once again, not without some controversy), and it went through fifteen editions in Watts's lifetime. It was later combined with *Hymns and Spiritual Songs* and published as *Hymns and Psalms*, a volume that sold more than fifty thousand copies per year for nearly a century and was said to have a greater impact on English life and thought than any other popular literature from the eighteenth century.[24]

Watts was truly an innovator in his *Psalms of David Imitated*, though he liked to pretend that he was not. He pointed back to other composers of metrical psalms in the seventeenth century, arguing that some of them had made similar modifications, but this argument is a little misleading, and Watts may have made it as a way to deflect criticism from the more radical nature of his project. One hymnographer to whom Watts appealed was John Patrick, whose *A Century of Selected Psalms* of 1679 had, in the words of Watts, "made use of the present language of Christianity . . . and left out many of the Judaisms."[25] In actual fact, neither Patrick nor any other predecessor went nearly as far as Watts did in his wholesale rewriting of the psalms.

More than half a century later, critics were still protesting Watts's work: "I am sure if David was to read [Watts's Psalms], he would not know any one of them to be his . . . The Scripture wants

23 Stevenson, "Dr. Watts' 'Flights of Fancy,'" 238–39; Hull, "Isaac Watts," 59–60; see also Davis, *Isaac Watts*, 199.

24 Davie, *Gathered Church*, 33–34.

25 Watts, *Psalms of David Imitated*, vi.

no mending."[26] It was made doubly controversial by the fact that Watts saw fit to omit a dozen psalms that he thought unworthy of paraphrase and unsuitable for Christian worship. In the end, though, Watts's method proved to be an enduringly popular way to render the psalms for congregational singing. Watts's collection became one of the most widespread hymnals of the eighteenth century and inspired several later imitations, including those by John Hughes and Samuel Say, by Charles Wesley, and by the noted Anglican poet Christopher Smart.[27]

The *Psalms of David Imitated* brought an end to Watts's major hymn-writing period (though a few more would appear in later collections of sermons and poetry), but not to his ministries of preaching and writing. He felt that his "system of praise" was well established through his two main volumes of hymns (*Hymns and Spiritual Songs* and *Psalms of David Imitated*), which he regarded as together being "a sufficient provision for psalmody, as to answer most occasions of the Christian life."[28]

Watts then shifted his primary focus to writing and teaching, aiming to encourage a revival of heartfelt devotion in Nonconformist churches. In doing so, he never lost his interest in issues of logic and the practice of education. He was an ardent defender of both the use of reason and the place of affective movements in the Christian life: in his own words, "the furniture of the head" must accompany the exercises of the heart.[29] He became known as a theologian and educator and was eventually recognized as an honorary Doctor of Divinity.

His work continued to be constrained by his frequent illnesses; some of his letters from the second half of his career reveal his gratitude at simply being able to stand in the pulpit for twenty minutes

26 Romaine, *Essay on Psalmody*, 137.

27 Bishop, *Isaac Watts*, xv; Marshall and Todd, *English Congregational Hymns*, 12.

28 Quoted in Rivers and Wykes, *Dissenting Praise*, 49.

29 Quoted in Sell, "Approaches," 271.

at a time.[30] He was involved in the doctrinal debates of his day and often tried to exercise a moderating influence. Some of his theological concerns centered on questions of Christology and Trinitarian theology raised by a few Nonconformist leaders who were shifting toward Unitarianism. In his attempts to find some middle ground with these thinkers, Watts occasionally stumbled into expressions of theology that deviated slightly from orthodox Trinitarianism. However, these issues do not seem to have influenced his legacy, perhaps because his hymns show no trace of such theological extemporizing.[31]

Until his death in 1748, he served as an inspiration and mentor to a new generation of Nonconformist ministers, among whom was a young pastor and hymnographer named Philip Doddridge. By the end of his life, he had secured a position as "the most prominent representative of Georgian Nonconformity" and held a "revered position in both English and American religion."[32]

Missiological Influences in Isaac Watts's Life

Isaac Watts, being greatly involved in the religious and social movements of his day, was no doubt impacted by many of the general influences in theology and missiology in early eighteenth-century England described in previous chapters. A few particulars, however, reveal themselves in his life, most prominently in his final two decades. It should be noted that most of the evidence of Watts's interest in the global expansion of Christianity comes not from his hymn-writing period but significantly afterward.

With regard to mission, most of Watts's attention was centered on developments among Native Americans in New England, as he maintained correspondence with clergy in that region for decades.

30 Bishop, *Isaac Watts*, xvi.

31 Orchard, *Nonconformity in Derbyshire*, 101; Stevenson, "Dr. Watts' 'Flights of Fancy,'" 248–51; Nicholls, *God and Government*, 154–55; Cousland, "Significance of Isaac Watts," 290–91.

32 Maclear, "Isaac Watts," 26; see also Cousland, "Significance of Isaac Watts," 289.

In 1737, Watts also noted with interest the news of revival in New England, one of the first movements of the Great Awakening.[33] This revival extended not only to English colonists but also to some Native American groups.

In fact, many of Watts's own writings had already been used in efforts to evangelize Native American tribes in New England, including his catechism for children and his *Psalms of David Imitated*.[34] Several workers in these missionary labors, including John Sergeant and David Brainerd, wrote about the influence of Watts's work upon their efforts. Sergeant noted, "If I may be thought to deserve in any measure the opinion of the world, it is not a little owing to the doctor's [that is, Isaac Watts's] ingenious writings, which have the force to charm minds to the love of piety and virtue."[35] Brainerd, who would become the most famous of this early generation of American missionaries, recorded in his journal his use of Watts's *Psalms of David Imitated* in his missionary work.[36] Similarly, Watts's hymns were distributed among many of the enslaved Africans in the colony of Virginia, where they were used effectively in teaching both literacy and the Christian faith.[37]

Watts became interested in these efforts and followed news of their progress. However, his habit of describing the North American revival and its effects as "surprising" suggests that he may not have developed a missiological sensibility as such, one which would have engaged in praying for or expecting the fruits of revival.[38] At the time of the North American revival, Watts's hymn-writing period had already largely ended, so it had no influence on the composition of his hymns. If it is a question of influence, the historical record shows that

---

33 Yeager, *Early Evangelicalism*, 5.

34 Beynon, *Isaac Watts: His Life*, 172–73.

35 Milner, *Life, Times, and Correspondence*, 539.

36 See Doddridge, *Abridgement*, 74.

37 Bond, *Poetic Wonder*, 68; King, "Psalms," 41–42.

38 See Hindmarsh, *Spirit of Early Evangelicalism*, 57.

Watts proved a greater influence on early missionary movements than they did on him.

The question remains, then: how missionally inclined was Watts during his hymn-writing period, roughly the decade and a half from 1705 to 1720? If his awareness of the revival and of missions to the Native Americans came after that, what can we say about his missiological reflections while he was writing his hymns? With the major exception of the *Psalms of David Imitated,* his other hymns do not paint a picture of someone with a compelling vision of global mission.

In much of his early writings, Watts was inclined to refer to non-Christian groups around the world—such as Turks, Indians, and Jews, or more generally, "heathens"—in a rhetorical fashion, as those who were so far from a true knowledge of the gospel that they could serve as a foil to contrast with the spiritual condition of English Christians. He does not appear to view them as objects of spiritual concern. For example, one of his hymns for children begins thus:

> Lord, I ascribe it to thy grace,
> And not to chance as others do,
> That I was born of Christian race,
> And not a heathen, or a Jew.[39]

This is not a hymn that has survived in modern usage, and for good reason—beyond the sheer offensiveness it entails for non-Christians, it reveals a certain callousness to the spiritual condition of others. Whereas we, from our perspective in a more mission-oriented age, would view "heathens" as the objects of God's love and desire their salvation, Watts shows no similar sensitivities. This kind of rhetoric reveals that Watts had not yet reached a point where he would likely consider launching missionary enterprises toward such people. Rather, in the face of heathenism's grip on many other nations, the best he can do is express gratitude that he was born in a Christian country, and not in an area without access to the gospel. Watts's expression shows

39 Watts, *Divine Songs,* 9.

an attitude not unlike that of the Pharisee in Jesus's parable of Luke 18:11 (NIV)—"God, I thank you that I am not like other people." It's fair to say that this is not the kind of hymn one would expect from a mission-minded hymnographer.

While the hymn above is probably the most egregious example in Watts's corpus of hymns, his other early works reinforce the sense that he was not inclined to think missionally. This can be seen in the two hymns he wrote on the Great Commission in his first major hymnbook, *Hymns and Spiritual Songs*. The first edition, in 1707, included one of these hymns, " 'Twas the Commission of the Lord," and Watts added a second one in his expanded edition of 1709: "'Go Preach My Gospel,' Saith the Lord." For most modern readers, a hymn on the Great Commission would quite naturally be expected to reflect on the missionary mandate of the church, but this is not what one finds in Watts's hymns. Here is the text for the first hymn, from 1707:

'Twas the commission of our Lord,
"Go, teach the nations, and baptize";
The nations have received the Word
Since he ascended to the skies.

He sits upon the eternal hills,
With grace and pardon in his hands,
And sends his covenant with the seals,
To bless the distant British lands.

"Repent, and be baptized," he saith,
For the remission of your sins;
And thus our sense assists our faith,
And shows us what his gospel means.

Our souls he washes in his blood,
As water makes the body clean;
And the good Spirit from our God
Descends like purifying rain.

Thus we engage ourselves to thee,
And seal our covenant with the Lord:
O may the great eternal Three
Confirm it at the heavenly board![40]

A few observations on this hymn: first, notice that the main application Watts makes is not about mission but about baptism. If someone is approaching this hymn and asking what it means for the ongoing life of the church, they would have to say that it paints a picture of baptism and personal commitment to the Lord. This is not atypical for a hymn on the Great Commission from this period; it was a biblical text most commonly cited with reference to baptism, not mission.

Second, where the hymn does mention global mission, its reference is to past history, not the present. Watts's immediate summary of the effects of the Great Commission is cast as a *fait accompli*: "The nations have received the Word / Since he ascended to the skies." While that may sound strange to our ears, knowing that Watts lived in an age when great swaths of the world had not yet received the gospel, it was a fairly common interpretation of the Great Commission in his own day. The missionary mandate of Christ was widely seen as having been given to the apostles in the first century and effectively completed (at least in an incipient sense) by their subsequent labors.[41] Watts even goes so far as to mention his own homeland, Britain, but as a recipient of missionary activity, not as a sending nation. Overall, his interpretation of the Great Commission leans away from any sense of duty or responsibility for the ongoing evangelization of the nations. The thought doesn't even seem to enter his mind.

But what about his second Great Commission hymn, from a couple years later? Here's the text of that piece:

---

40 Watts, *Hymns and Spiritual Songs*, 51.

41 See LaGrand, *Earliest Christian Mission*, 235; Parris, *Reading the Bible*, 15; Bosch, "Structure of Mission," 218.

"Go preach my gospel," saith the LORD;
"Bid the whole Earth my grace receive;
He shall be saved that trusts my Word,
He shall be damned that won't believe.

"I'll make your great commission known,
And ye shall prove my gospel true
By all the works that I have done,
By all the wonders ye shall do.

"Go heal the sick, go raise the dead,
Go cast out devils in my name;
Nor let my prophets be afraid,
Though Greeks reproach and Jews blaspheme.

"Teach all the nations my commands,
I'm with you till the world shall end;
All power is trusted to my hands,
can destroy, and I defend."

He spoke, and light shone round his head,
On a bright cloud to heaven he rode;
They to the farthest nations spread
The grace of their ascended GOD.[42]

At first glance, this hymn might look more promising. It isn't focused on baptism, like the previous hymn, but appears to give attention to the methods and means of apostolic evangelism. At the very least, it is interested in the missional aspects of the Great Commission, even if an application to Watts's own day is still in question. In fact, this hymn is significant for at least one reason that should be of interest to mission-minded Christians: as far as we can tell, this is where the name "Great Commission" originated as a reference to the closing verses of Matthew's Gospel. The term, which Watts uses in verse 2 of his hymn, is unknown prior to its appearance

42 Watts, *Hymns and Spiritual Songs*, 2nd ed., 101–2.

here, at least in English (there is a prior possible usage from a Dutch missionary, Justinian von Welz). As far as we know, then, Watts coined the English term "Great Commission" with reference to this passage.[43]

Readers might also look at the opening line of verse 3—"I'll make your great commission known"—and think they see an intentionally missionary spirit represented there. It sounds like a statement of resolution, after all, a pledge to spread the knowledge of the gospel far and wide. Unfortunately, that's not actually what the line is saying. Verse 3 is not represented as the voice of the Christian singing the hymn, but rather as the voice of Jesus speaking to his disciples. Watts's use of punctuation in the hymn makes it clear that the entire text, except the last verse, is a paraphrase of Jesus's words. So when it says, "I'll make your great commission known," this is not a mandate for the singing Christian to claim but is intended as a statement Jesus makes to the disciples. Essentially, it is just Jesus saying to his first-century apostles, "Listen up, now I'm giving you your assignment."

From that point on, readers will notice that every aspect of the missionary methods described is put in the context of the apostolic missions of the first century. If that isn't already clear with verse 4's references to apostolic miracles and ministry among Greeks and Jews, the final verse makes it abundantly clear: "They to the farthest nations spread / The grace of their ascended God." Again, as in the previous hymn, it seems that Watts sees the Great Commission as primarily applying to the original disciples and fulfilled by their labors.

Still, the fact that Watts devotes an entire hymn to the subject is important. The apostolic mission is held up as inspiring, empowering, and effective. Even if Watts does not take the step of applying the Great Commission as an ongoing command to himself and his contemporaries, the attention he pays to it would nonetheless have an effect on the congregations that sang it regularly. Eventually, perhaps, such a congregation might come to see the apostolic mission as

43 Wright, "Great Commission," 153–54; cf. Castleman, "Last Word," 68.

worthy of emulation, especially in the face of a world that still needed a gospel witness in its "farthest nations."

Both of these hymns on the Great Commission, though, came several years before Watts's infamous children's hymn celebrating the fact that he wasn't born a heathen. On balance, one is forced to admit that Watts, especially in his early period, was not a particularly missional thinker. Where he engages with mission-oriented Scripture texts, like the Great Commission, he tends to view them either with reference to baptism or to their fulfillment in the first-century apostolic missions.

In Watts's case, it is possible to judge the matter not only from his hymns but also from his other writings. Even in his later periods, after the release of *Psalms of David Imitated,* he does not devote much attention to the question of global Christian mission. He has an interest in the revivals and the local missions to the Native Americans in New England, but he does not typically set these interests in the context of a larger expectation of continued missions around the world, at least not in the immediate future. His interest lies mostly in the fact that curious things were happening among his Congregationalist communion. Congregationalists were a small and little-regarded group in England, so to see them flourishing across the Atlantic was a sight that naturally drew his attention. Unfortunately, it seems that Watts never developed a well-honed sense of the church's missionary mandate.

This makes it all the more startling when we turn our attention to Watts's 1719 hymnbook, *The Psalms of David Imitated,* where the call for global missions rings out from nearly every page. This hymnbook would go on—sometimes on its own, and sometimes in a dual edition with *Hymns and Spiritual Songs*—to become the most popular hymnal of the eighteenth century's "Golden Age of Hymns."[44] Its frequent use and its strong missional sensibilities ended up paving the way for the

44 See Davie, *Gathered Church,* 33–34.

launch of the Protestant mission movement in the 1790s. Where, then, did it come from? How did such a non-missional thinker as Isaac Watts end up writing such a text? The next chapter turns its attention to those very questions.

5

Awaken, Harp and Lyre!

The Psalms Reimagined

The publication of Watts's new version of the biblical psalms in 1719 was one of those unremarkable events in church history that, in retrospect, has profoundly shaped subsequent generations of Christians. In its own day, it attracted considerable attention, being lauded by some and criticized by others. Yet most of that early focus was on whether Watts's grand project of interpolating Old Testament Scripture into Christianized paraphrases was appropriate. Other issues—including those that would have a lasting impact—went unnoticed at first. Chief among these was the little-noted fact that Watts's new hymnbook subtly introduced a deeply missional vein of reflection into congregational song.

More than a decade into his hymn-writing program, Watts issued the *Psalms of David Imitated*, his second (and final) major hymnbook intended for regular congregational worship. His first significant foray, *Hymns and Spiritual Songs*, had been better received than he expected, which led to an expanded edition of that work.[1] There were some critics of his program, as was to be expected. But Watts was aware of those challenges beforehand, and his essay attached to *Hymns and Spiritual Songs* laid out the reasons for his position. Christians should be able to sing about Jesus, he argued, and have songs that celebrate the gospel of grace revealed in Christ's work of salvation. He was not

1 See Benson, *English Hymn*, 116–17; Bishop, *Isaac Watts*, xxxiii; Phillips, *Hymnal*, 88.

intent on removing psalmody from churches but rather on introducing an "improvement of psalmody," so that Christians would have access to songs that fit the spiritual and emotional character of their faith.

Now it was 1719, a decade after the definitive second edition of *Hymns and Spiritual Songs* was published. The full title of Watts's new hymnbook was *The Psalms of David Imitated in the Language of the New Testament, and Applied to the Christian State and Worship*. Instead of moving further away from the use of the biblical psalms in worship, he presented this book as a return to them . . . sort of. It went back to the psalms but cast them into an entirely new form, transforming the content of each psalm into Christian material.

This was a daring and controversial project, to say the least. At first glance, one might think that Watts's critics would be comforted to see that the psalms were still being incorporated into the sung worship of the church. But the real difficulty came with the realization that Watts was taking biblical content and modifying it in ways that made the original scarcely recognizable.[2] For most people, though, the appeal of Watts's *Psalms of David Imitated* outweighed any concerns they had about his handling of Scripture.

Watts could foresee most of the critiques before they were voiced, and he addressed them in his accompanying writings. It would be one thing if he were presenting his hymns as versions of the biblical text, but he was not. They were hymns, not psalms, created as imitations and homages to the originals, but making no pretense of claiming divine inspiration for their text. Further, as most of Watts's audience recognized, his imitations of the psalms were theologically orthodox and poetically compelling. One might object to the audacity of the project, but the actual content of the work appeared to be above reproach in terms of the theology conveyed. In fact, the broad reception of the work was enthusiastic, and it immediately caught on in Nonconformist churches both in England and North America.[3]

2 See, for example, Romaine, *Essay on Psalmody*, 137.

3 See Phillips, "Cotton Mather," 206.

So how did Watts go about writing songs for this new hymnbook? Metrical psalters typically had one hymn per psalm, matching the original exactly, which often resulted in absurdly long hymns. Watts's hymnbook, by contrast, broke many of the psalms up, offering multiple different hymns for each psalm, such that his pieces (while still long by today's standards) were more amenable to congregational singing. At times, he wrote multiple different versions based on the same passage, giving congregations more options for choosing the setting they liked best. He also made use of common poetic meters, paired with well-known tunes, to make the transition easier.

Watts's method of transposing the psalms had two major steps. First, he examined the content of each psalm and asked, "How would David have written this psalm if he had lived in the New Testament era?" or more precisely, "What if David had known all that we know about the gospel?" That question infused a new layer of meaning to each psalm, incorporating references to Jesus, the Holy Spirit, the church, and the Christian life, which enriched the longings and expectations of David's ancient songs. In the second step, Watts arranged this content into metered lines so it could be sung. His hymns would not always cover all the content of a given psalm, but the amount of biblical content represented is impressive nonetheless. Here's one of his versions of Psalm 2 (only the part corresponding to Psalm 2:1–6 is included here, but the full hymn covers the entirety of the psalm):

Psalm 2:1–6 (KJV)	Watts's Hymn on Psalm 2
Why do the heathen rage, and the people imagine a vain thing? The kings of the earth set themselves, and the rulers take counsel together, against the LORD, and against his anointed,	Why did the Jews proclaim their rage? The Romans why their swords employ? Against the Lord their powers engage His dear Anointed to destroy.

saying, Let us break their bands asunder, and cast away their cords from us.	"Come, let us break his bands," they say, "This man shall never give us laws"; And thus they cast his yoke away, And nailed the Monarch to the Cross.
He that sitteth in the heavens shall laugh: the LORD shall have them in derision. Then shall he speak unto them in his wrath, and vex them in his sore displeasure.	But God who high in glory reigns Laughs at their pride, their rage controls; He'll vex their hearts with inward pains, And speak in thunder to their souls.
Yet have I set my king upon my holy hill of Zion.	"I will maintain the King I made On Zion's everlasting hill, My hand shall bring him from the dead, And he shall stand your Sovereign still."[4]

As you can see in this example, Watts uses all the material of the underlying psalm and expands upon it by interpreting it with a view toward the crucifixion of Jesus. Most of the hymns in *Psalms of David Imitated* follow this pattern, providing fairly comprehensive coverage of the biblical material. However, Watts doesn't just repeat the content of the psalm; otherwise, the centuries-long tradition of metrical psalters would have infused significant missiological content into English Christian worship. Watts includes another part of the process: re-imagining the biblical content in Christian terminology. It is here that the transfiguration of the psalms' missiology becomes apparent.

To illustrate the difference between the two methods of turning psalms into hymns—the metrical psalter method and Watts's "imitations"—it is worth comparing Watts's efforts with those of previous psalters. Watts's *Psalms of David Imitated* was a truly daring enterprise, a new and controversial idea, but even he appealed to the tradition of metrical psalters to argue that his project was not as radical as it might seem. Nevertheless, his work stands out as being different in several notable respects, not least of which is the transposition of the biblical missiology of the psalms into a Christian key.

4 Watts, *Psalms of David Imitated*, 8.

Watts specifically notes the prior work of Dr. John Patrick, who, he says, already produced a psalter that referenced Christian themes.[5] What Watts doesn't openly admit is that the vast majority of Patrick's work is a straightforward metrical translation, with only passing references to Christ or the church scattered here and there. Thus, Patrick's psalms are not really a significant antecedent to Watts's work. In the chart below, Watts's version of Psalm 19 is compared to its parallel texts in Patrick's volume and in Nicholas Tate and Nahum Brady's "New Version," the standard psalter of the day. The bold print indicates where Watts has introduced new material that shifts the psalm in a missional direction:

John Patrick (1679)	**Tate & Brady (1696)**	**Isaac Watts (1719)**
The heavens, whose beauteous frame we see, / God's skill and power proclaim; [...] / These though they have no voice like ours, / Nor words to them belong; / Yet they express to all the World / Thy praise, without a tongue. [...] / Forth from the eastern coast he [the sun] bends / His course unto the west: / All the Earth rejoices in his light, / And by his heat is blest.[6]	The heavens declare thy glory, Lord, / The firmament and stars express their great Creator's skill. [...] / Their powerful language to no realm or region is confined, / 'Tis nature's voice, and understood alike by all mankind. / Their doctrine does its sacred sense through Earth's extent display; [...] / From east to west, from west to east, his restless course he [the sun] goes, / And through his progress cheerful light and vital warmth bestows.[7]	The heavens declare thy glory, Lord, / In every star thy wisdom shines: [...] / Sun, moon, and stars convey thy praise / Round the whole Earth, and never stand: / So when thy truth begun its race, / It touched and glanced on every land. / **Nor shall thy spreading gospel rest, / Till through the world thy truth has run; / Till Christ has all the nations blest,** / That see the light, or feel the sun.[8]

5 Watts, vi.

6 Patrick, *Century of Select Psalms*, 17.

7 Tate and Brady, *New Version*, 28.

8 Watts, *Psalms of David Imitated*, 56–57.

This example illustrates the missiological transformations that Watts produces when he engages both steps of his method. While translating the psalm into a singable form, much like other metrical versions, he also seeks ways to convey its content as if it had been written with a full Christian understanding of the gospel. Here, he takes the idea of the "doctrine" (to use Tate and Brady's term) that the sun, moon, and stars proclaim all around the earth—namely, the wisdom and skill of God's work of creation—and asks what a corresponding doctrine would be in the Christian age, something that is to be proclaimed to every land. The answer he arrives at, quite naturally, is the message of the good news of Jesus, and so he uses the psalm's idea of the global proclamation of God's truth to introduce the concept of the gospel being proclaimed to all nations. This is not an idea that appeared in the metrical psalters that preceded Watts, as they adhered more closely to the literal meaning of the biblical psalms, and so Watts's work represents an entirely new infusion of missiological thought into the songs of the church.

In most cases, aside from the transfiguration of certain statements in a Christward sense, Watts tends to follow the structure of a given psalm fairly closely. In other cases, though, the connection between the underlying psalmic material and his finished product is less apparent, but it is still present. Consider his hymn "Jesus Shall Reign," based on Psalm 72, in which he not only interprets the text in a Christian direction but also elides some portions and shuffles the order of others:

Psalm 72 (KJV)	"Jesus Shall Reign" (Watts)
- [The king] shall have dominion also from sea to sea […] (v. 8) - They shall fear thee as long as the sun and moon endure, throughout all generations (v. 5) - […] his name shall be continued as long as the sun (v. 17) - […] so long as the moon endureth (v. 7)	Jesus shall reign where e'er the sun Does his successive journeys run; His kingdom stretch from shore to shore, Till moons shall wax and wane no more.

- The kings of Tarshish and of the isles shall bring presents: the kings of Sheba and Seba shall offer gifts. Yea, all kings shall fall down before him: all nations shall serve him. (vv. 10–11)	Behold the islands with their kings, And Europe her best tribute brings; From north to south the princes meet To pay their homage at his feet.
- They that dwell in the wilderness shall bow before him; and his enemies shall lick the dust (v. 9) - *(See also the passage associated with Verse 2 of the hymn, above)*	There Persia glorious to behold, There India shines in eastern gold; And barbarous nations at his word Submit and bow and own their Lord.
- […] prayer also shall be made for him continually; and daily shall he be praised (v. 15) - And blessed be his glorious name for ever […] (v. 19)	For him shall endless prayer be made And praises throng to crown his head; His name like sweet perfume shall rise With every morning sacrifice.
- […] all nations shall call him blessed (v. 17) - *(See also the passages associated with verse 4 of the hymn)*	People and realms of every tongue Dwell on his love with sweetest song; And infant voices shall proclaim Their early blessings on his name.
- For he shall deliver the needy when he crieth; the poor also, and him that hath no helper. He shall spare the poor and needy, and shall save the souls of the needy. (vv. 12–13)	Blessings abound where e'er he reigns, The prisoner leaps to lose his chains, The weary find eternal rest, And all the sons of want are blest.
- […] men shall be blessed in him (v. 17) - He shall redeem their soul from deceit and violence […] (v. 14) - *(See also the passages associated with verse 6 of the hymn, above)*	Where he displays his healing power, Death and the curse are known no more; In him the tribes of Adam boast More blessings than their father lost.
- […] all nations shall call him blessed (v. 17) - And blessed be his glorious name for ever: and let the whole earth be filled with his glory; Amen, and Amen. (v. 19)	Let every creature rise and bring, Peculiar honours to our king; Angels descend with songs again, And Earth repeat the long Amen.[9]

9 Watts, *Psalms of David Imitated*, 186–87.

Watts's arrangement of the biblical material, then, is subject to his own judgment. But despite his practices of changing the order and reimagining elements of the psalm in a Christian sense, the content is still clearly inspired by the underlying psalm. Every single stanza of the hymn is rooted in some portion of the original psalm. Even in hymns where the connection to the underlying text is looser—like his transformation of Psalm 98 into "Joy to the World"—the outline of the biblical psalm still provides the framework for the entire hymn. The important point, then, is that the selection of topic, content, and theme is a responsibility that Watts concedes to the biblical psalms; his work is simply to reimagine that content in a specifically Christian sense.

In the case of "Jesus Shall Reign," this method of transforming the psalm results in a vision of all nations bringing their worship before Christ. Whereas the original psalm shows an Israelite king—perhaps Solomon—receiving tribute and honor from distant regional powers, Watts identifies Jesus as the king. Even more strikingly, he replaces the names of the ancient regional powers—Tarshish, Sheba, and Seba—with areas from his own contemporary world: Europe, Persia, and India. For the latter two areas, this image would have been startling to Watts's audience: Persia and India, known as stubborn bastions of non-Christian religions, bowing down in worship to Jesus. (Even the reference to Europe may have been striking for Watts's low-church Protestant audience, as it would have conjured visions of Catholic and Orthodox believers submitting to the lordship of Christ—something that, from their perspective, might have seemed surprising at the time.)

Notice, however, that the missional vision of "Jesus Shall Reign" is not really the product of any special efforts on Watts's part—like all the other hymns in the *Psalms of David Imitated*, it is simply the theology of underlying psalm, transfigured with Christian and contemporary references. He likely chose Persia and India simply because they fit his practice of changing ancient references into contemporary ones, selecting areas that were both distant yet prominent in the minds of his English audience (particularly in the early days of Britain's trade empire, when British geopolitical connections in India and Persia were just beginning to grow). Although his audience would have been struck by the missiological implications of the vision he paints, that probably wasn't Watts's main intention in his word choice; he was simply following his method.

In short, most of Watts's missiological references in these hymns appear to come from two sources: first, from the underlying missiology of the biblical psalms, and second, as unintentional byproducts of his methodology. The biblical missiology inherent in the psalms is pervasive but not necessarily linked to an active sense of Christian vision—it is more often presented as a prophetic call to the nations to join in the worship of God. It is only through the application of Watts's methodology that this underlying missiological vision is transformed into a more active sense, aligning with the proclamation of the gospel to the nations. However, as we've seen from our survey of Watts's other hymns and his broader body of work, his thought was not particularly inclined toward a global vision of Christian mission. The rich missiology of the *Psalms of David Imitated* seems to confirm this, being a combination of biblical missiology and the providential accident of his hymn-writing method, rather than arising from Watts's own missiological reflections.

Consider one more example of Watts's method of turning psalms into Christian hymns. The hymn below is Watts's version of Psalm 117, the shortest in the Book of Psalms:

Psalm 117 (KJV)	**Watts's Hymn on Psalm 117**
O praise the LORD, all ye nations: praise him, all ye people.	O all ye nations, praise the LORD, Each with a different tongue; In every language learn his Word, And let his name be sung.
For his merciful kindness is great toward us: and the truth of the LORD endureth for ever. Praise ye the Lord.	His mercy reigns through every land; Proclaim his grace abroad; Forever firm his truth shall stand; Praise ye the faithful God.[10]

10 Watts, 305.

This is one of the most mission-oriented hymns in Watts's *Psalms of David Imitated*, but again, note that the content is inspired by the underlying missiology of the biblical psalm. Here, however, we can see more clearly some of the providential accidents of Watts's hymn-writing method, which tended to amplify the missiology of the psalm in ways that Watts himself likely did not foresee. While there is some implicit missiology in the psalm—a global view of all nations worshiping the Lord—Watts's hymn expands on this idea in a few notable ways. First, he introduces the concept of many different languages praising God in verse 1, and in verse 2 he includes what is perhaps the most missional-sounding line in his entire corpus: "Proclaim his grace abroad." The missional sound of this line, however, is largely due to a curious misreading of the text.

The object of address in Psalm 117 is *the nations*, as introduced in the opening line. This is paralleled in Hebrew by a following reference to "all peoples" (in the KJV above, "all ye people")—again, with the object of address being all the people of the world. When the psalm adds a self-reference in the next section—"us"—the psalmist is not only speaking of himself or his own worshiping community but of the whole company of humanity, all addressed together. This also seems to be Watts's understanding in his rendering of the hymn—there is only one object of address named in the hymn, and that is *the nations*—"O all ye nations." In Watts's version, he even drops the "us," implying that he is still addressing the nations when he gets to verse 2. As such, the line "Proclaim his grace abroad" is not a charge given to the worshipers singing the hymn (as many people naturally read it); rather, it is a charge that Watts directs to all the nations. That is to say, he does not appear to assign any extra sense of duty or intentionality to the work of global missions here, as if it were the responsibility of the congregation singing the hymn to proclaim God's grace abroad—that charge is directed at the nations themselves.

Despite Watts's intentions, however, there is good reason to believe that his audience likely understood that line as a charge addressed to themselves and interpreted it in an active, missional sense. This is because the implied addressee of the charge—the nations—had been referenced back at the beginning of verse 1. There's significant distance between the beginning of verse 1 and the middle of verse 2, even in a normal singing style. However, when used in the common practice of "lining out"—as many of Watts's hymns would have first been sung—that distance is effectively doubled by repetitions from the worship leader and the congregation. By the time the congregation reaches the charge to "Proclaim his grace abroad," they most likely would have forgotten that it was originally addressed to all the peoples of the earth in the abstract and would take it as a command directed at themselves. In this way, by a sheer accident of the hymn's construction, the subdued missiology of the psalm is transformed into something active and intentional, directly engaging the reader or singer.

Other features of the hymn seem to share similar providential accidents. The psalm is so short, for example, that Watts has to add a significant amount of material just to fill out two stanzas. This leads him, in verse 1, to start looking for an end rhyme with "sung," which results in the introduction of a new missiological theme: the idea of God's word being learned in all the tongues and languages of the world. To be clear, that theme is not explicitly present in the original psalm, nor is it an idea that appears elsewhere in Watts's writings (the idea of translating the gospel message into other languages so that God's praise can reach all nations)—it seems to be a happy accident forced upon him by his hymn-writing method. The same pattern re-emerges in verse 2: the line "proclaim his grace abroad" is not directly based on the underlying psalm; it seems to be Watts's addition to provide an end rhyme matching the final line's concluding reference to God. And while that line might strike us as an intentional charge to missional activity, it should be emphasized again that we find no other evidence for that kind of intentional sense of responsibility in Watts's works—not even, for the most part, in the rest of his *Psalms of David Imitated*. So these additions to Psalm 117, which strike us as resoundingly missiological, are most likely just poetic fillers that Watts employed to round out the underlying message of the biblical psalm.

Over and over, throughout the *Psalms of David Imitated,* the same pattern re-emerges. The implicit missiology of the psalms, with its grand vision of all nations praising God, is transfigured by Watts's methodology and cast into a vision of all nations coming to know the gospel of Jesus Christ. This pattern is particularly evident in a set of hymns Watts writes on Psalms 96 and 97, in which the rhetoric of the gospel's spread to all nations is so clear that Watts felt it necessary to include an explanatory footnote. He evidently struggled with how to render these psalms, because his initial sense was that they related to the Last Judgment, but he also noted that they were full of joyful overtones. Since Watts associated the Last Judgment with dread rather than with joy, he decided to introduce references to Christ's first coming in order to represent the joy of the psalms and then transition to Christ's second coming in the final verses. To match the psalm's singular focus, however (apparently referencing just one coming of the Lord), Watts said that he had to represent "the first coming of Christ into the world [...] in a prophetic style, as though he were coming a second time to the Last Judgment."[11]

This means that Watts presents the idea of spreading the gospel in a "prophetic style" of expression, calling the nations to faith in Christ, acknowledging both his first coming and preparing for his second. Watts writes these hymns similarly to how the psalms and certain prophetic books of the Bible address the nations rhetorically (much as in Psalm 117—"O praise the LORD, all ye nations," or in Psalm 67's subjunctive call to "Let the nations be glad"). These biblical passages were probably not implying an active and intentional missiology, suggesting that Israelite missionaries should go out and actively bring about gladness among the nations. Instead, they were simply a form of rhetorical address directed to those nations as part of the prophetic writings of the Israelite canon.

11 Watts, 248.

Watts decides to use this prophetic-rhetorical form to turn the psalms' content into references to Christ's first and second comings, resulting in some of the most richly missiological expressions found in all his hymns. Consider the following lines from his hymns based on Psalms 96 and 97 (these excerpts are from the opening sections, not the entirety of either hymn):

> Sing to the Lord, ye distant lands,
> Ye tribes of every Tongue;
> His new-discovered grace demands
> A new and nobler song.
> Say to the nations, Jesus reigns,
> God's own almighty Son;
> His power the sinking world sustains,
> And grace surrounds his throne.
>
> Let all the Earth their voices raise
> To sing the choicest psalm of praise,
> To sing and bless Jehovah's name:
> His glory let the heathens know,
> His wonders to the nations show,
> And all his saving works proclaim.
> The heathens know thy glory, Lord;
> The wondering nations read thy Word.[12]

These lines contain several prophetic and rhetorical addresses to the nations (set in both active and subjunctive forms) as well as an anticipatory vision of all nations, having received the gospel and the Word of God, being prepared for his second coming. Notice, however, that Watts still doesn't use an intentional sense of Christan responsibility to enact this spread of the gospel (though the line "Say to the nations, Jesus reigns" can be mistaken as such when read at a glance, instead of its actual function as a prophetic call). This lack of active intentionality regarding global mission is a characteristic

12 Watts, 247–48.

feature of Watts's hymns and marks one of the main differences between his missiological themes and those in Philip Doddridge's hymns, written some three decades later.

Furthermore, the sheer fact that Watts felt it necessary to include a long footnote explaining his method of rendering these hymns suggests that he regarded such expressions to be atypical, something that would spark questions in his audience. For most modern readers, these hymns probably wouldn't raise such questions, as we are used to thinking about a global-sized vision of the spread of the gospel, but apparently, that was not the case in Watts's day. He felt he must explain himself, which indicates just how little missiological content they were accustomed to seeing in their hymns.

Having said that, and taking into account Watts's own limitations regarding his missiological vision—these hymns are still powerfully missional! Watts appears not to have anticipated the effects that would flow from his hymns, but it is hard to imagine a congregation singing these joyful songs week after week, year after year, without developing a profoundly missional view of the world. Watts managed to write hymns that would reshape the entire sense Christians had of the scope and scale of the evangelistic charge on their lives, all while being blissfully unaware this that would be their effect.

This, then, suggests the work of the Holy Spirit in shaping and using this particular moment in church history. The more we recognize the missional power of Watts's hymns, coupled with his own apparent lack of vision and intentionality, the more the "providential accidents" I've been describing begin to look like providence, rather than mere accidents.

In many ways, Watts is an unlikely candidate for fostering a new sense of missional awareness in Nonconformist church culture. When writing hymns whose content was derived from his own creative process (as in his earlier hymnbooks), the result was songs that applied the Great Commission to Jesus's disciples, rather than to subsequent generations of Christians. His clearest reference to unreached people groups was a line where English children gave thanks to God for not being born a "heathen" or a Jew.

But his *Psalms of David Imitated* produced something strikingly different, partly because the content of the songs was not dependent on his own creative impulses. Rather, he drew on the underlying content of Scripture. Although he modified the words of the psalms and adjusted their content to align with New Testament themes, it was still the theology of the psalms that set the direction for Watts's new songs. And so this profoundly un-missional thinker took the underlying missiology of the biblical psalms and considered what it would sound like if it was rendered into the theology of the Christian gospel. As a result, the psalms' call for all nations to praise the Lord became a call for every nation to hear and respond to the gospel of Jesus Christ. By the time he was finished, Isaac Watts had produced one of the most mission-oriented hymnals in all of church history, all while being largely unaware of the significance of his output.

In the dissertation research that inspired this book, the statistical results for missiological themes in Watts's *Psalms of David Imitated* constituted a significant outlier when compared to every other Nonconformist hymnbook in the first half-century of the Golden Age of Hymns (including Watts's other works). When removing the *Psalms of David Imitated* from the results, one could trace a slight but gradual rise in missiological content in major Nonconformist hymnbooks from the years 1706 to 1755. However, including the *Psalms of David Imitated* produced a wild and erratic spike in the middle of the chart. This one hymnbook contained far more missiological content in its lines than any of the other works, with three to four times as many references.

Why should we attribute this to the Spirit's guidance? First, because the hymns in question were based on the inspired texts of Scripture. In any case where the biblical message is being presented in a faithful manner, one can expect the Spirit to be at work. Second, the missiological emphasis of the psalms was brought to the forefront when cast in the light of the gospel. Watts was reflecting on Old Testament revelation through the lens of Jesus Christ—the very activity for which the writers of the New Testament claimed and expected the Spirit's guidance. Third, natural causation does not seem to be a sufficient explanation for the thematic trend in this hymnbook, since the author's own predisposition toward questions of global mission appears to have run in the opposite direction, or at least to have been significantly underdeveloped compared to his hymns. And fourth, the results that flowed from this new movement in hymnody speak to a fresh move of God among the Nonconformist churches. As the missional hymns of Isaac Watts became the songs of the church, week after week and decade after decade, those very same churches began to show a more robust sense of missional responsibility, until they leapt onto the stage of world history as the vanguard of the Protestant mission movement.

At every turn in this story, one is struck by how unexpected this should be—one wouldn't expect Watts to write missional hymns like these, nor would one expect the Nonconformists to rise from their insular obscurity to become the leading players of a world-shaping mission revolution. Yet both things happened. The marked rise in the missiological content of this hymnbook, along with the fact that the churches singing from it were the same ones to launch a global mission movement just a few decades later, all suggest that a serendipity of grace was at work behind the scenes. While a historian cannot prove that the divine hand has been at work in history in such a particular way, the suggestion must at least be raised.

6

Philip Doddridge
The Missionary Spirit Enshrined in Song

If the first transformational touchstone in this story of hymns and missions was Watts's 1719 *Psalms of David Imitated*, the second would be the life and work of Philip Doddridge, whose hymns were published posthumously in 1755. Doddridge, like Watts, was a Congregationalist, and he was directly inspired by his predecessor's contributions to hymnody. But while Watts was, at best, an unintentional mission-hymn writer, Doddridge's hymns elevated the missiological content to new heights of clear-eyed vision and intentionality. In fact, if any English Nonconformist can be pointed to as a man before his time, anticipating the developments in missional thinking that would emerge at the end of the century, it would be Philip Doddridge.[1]

There were a few other Nonconformist hymnographers who made contributions in the decades between Watts and Doddridge—Joseph Stennett, Simon Browne, Daniel Turner, and Benjamin Wallin—but none had the widespread impact of either Watts or Doddridge.[2] The only comparable hymnographers of the time were those active in other communions, like John and Charles Wesley, who wrote hymns for their Methodist/Anglican movement. The Wesleys' hymns, while notable in their own right, are not considered

1 Reynolds and Price, *Survey of Christian Hymnody*, 50.

2 See Phillips, *Hymnal*, 87–88; Benson, *English Hymn*, 212–13; cf. Wainwright and Westerfield Tucker, *Oxford History of Christian Worship*, 565–67.

here because they played a lesser early role in shaping Nonconformist thought through hymnody.[3] Their movement only gradually became associated with other Nonconformist churches, and they lagged a decade or two behind the Baptists and Congregationalists at the launch of the Protestant mission movement. Even though the Methodists certainly had the theological tools to build a mission movement—one of their leaders, Thomas Coke, even wrote a significant missiological treatise several years before William Carey's—they were still a step or two behind the Nonconformists at the end of the eighteenth century.[4] All things considered, then, in the first wave of the Golden Age of Hymns, it was Watts and Doddridge, the great Nonconformist hymnographers, who stand out as noteworthy figures in the rising tide of missional reflection.

Philip Doddridge did not achieve the same high level of public recognition as Watts in hymnography, though he was still well-known and influential in his own day. While his hymns had a moderate impact on the growing field of Nonconformist hymnody, he was also widely regarded for his prose writings and ministerial labors. One of his books, *The Rise and Progress of Religion in the Soul*, would come to be regarded as a classic of the early evangelical movement and played a significant part in the history of English Christianity (not least by its role in the conversion of William Wilberforce, the famous anti-slavery reformer).[5]

Despite not quite matching Watts's popularity, Doddridge's work in hymnody was still significantly more influential than any of the other Nonconformist figures writing hymns at the time. He occupied a tier all his own, with Watts above him and with Simon Browne and the minor Baptist hymnographers well below. Indeed, Doddridge's volume of hymns, published posthumously by his associate Job Orton in 1755,

3 See Marini, "Hymnody as History," 274–75; Benson, *English Hymn*, 258–59; Bailey, *Gospel in Hymns*, 66–67.

4 See Stanley, *History of the Baptist Missionary Society*, 2; Beeching, *Open Path*, 68; Bosch, *Transforming Mission*, 285.

5 Carter, "Philip Doddridge," 31.

was quickly accepted as a supplement to the hymns of Watts then in circulation and enjoyed widespread use alongside Watts's collections.[6]

The Life of Philip Doddridge

Philip Doddridge was born in London in 1702, and, like Watts, his familial roots in Nonconformism ran deep. Both of his grandfathers had been persecuted for their beliefs: one had been a Puritan-Anglican clergyman until the Act of Uniformity forced him out of the ministry; the other had been a Hussite who was expelled from his homeland in Bohemia after the Hapsburg conquest in 1636.[7] Doddridge and his family experienced other sufferings beyond religious persecution—both of his parents died while he was a teenager. In Doddridge's own words, these tragedies occured when he was "at an age in which it might reasonably be supposed a child should be most sensible of such a loss."[8] Thankfully, it was also an age at which he could easily be taken under the wing of his educators at the dissenting schools he attended. He eventually ended up at Saint Albans, where he came under the care of Rev. Samuel Clark, a Congregational minister.[9]

Like Watts, Doddridge faced an important choice when he became old enough to choose where to further his studies, whether at one of the great universities or at a dissenting academy. In Doddridge's case, there were significant stakes attached to his choice, because he had received an offer from an old benefactor of his uncle's, the Duchess of Bedford, who said she would pay for his education should he pursue studies to serve the Church of England. Again like Watts, Doddridge chose conscience over the stability of secure finances and social favor. He left the Duchess's offer on the table and instead enrolled in a dissenting academy in Kibworth, Leicestershire, in 1719.[10]

---

6 Benson, *English Hymn*, 212.

7 Matthews, *Calamy Revised*, 166.

8 Doddridge, *Sermons to Young Persons*, 158.

9 Strivens, *Philip Doddridge*, 2.

10 Carter, "Philip Doddridge," 29.

Following the counsel of his mentor Samuel Clark, and after a long period of thought and prayer, he resolved to study for the ministry and to enter the service of a Congregational church. He wrote:

> I have sought God's direction in this matter, and I hope I have had it. My only view in my choice hath been that of more extensive service; and I beg God would make me an instrument of doing much good in the world.[11]

After his studies at Kibworth, he began serving in pastoral ministry in the same town, though only in a part-time role. In 1730 he moved to Northampton and undertook the pastorate of the Congregational church at Castle Hill. The Castle Hill church would be the seat of his ministry for the next two decades, until his death in 1751.[12]

While in Northampton, Doddridge expanded on some small-scale teaching he had been doing and started tutoring prospective young ministers in their studies. He was entering the ministry at a time when Nonconformists felt their movement was at a low ebb. Theologically liberalizing trends in Presbyterianism and among General Baptists had sapped their strength, and their numbers had declined significantly—issues which Doddridge felt he needed to address.[13] The early 1730s saw the beginning of his writing career, and he soon became widely known for several prominent works, including his *Course of Lectures* for ministry students, his *Family Expositor*, a Bible commentary designed for use in family devotions, and his popular devotional treatise, *The Rise and Progress of Religion in the Soul*.

The latter work, *Rise and Progress*, underscores the connections between Isaac Watts and Philip Doddridge, as the idea for the book originated with Watts, who passed the project to his younger colleague when it became clear that his own weak health would prevent him

11 Orton, *Memoirs*, 14.

12 Strivens, *Philip Doddridge*, 2–3.

13 See Doddridge, *Free Thoughts*, 199–224; Chute, Finn, and Haykin, *Baptist Story*, 71–72.

from writing it.[14] However, Doddridge included some thoughts in the text that Watts would probably not have considered: *Rise and Progress* contains one of the first clear calls from an English Nonconformist to intentionally engage in the work of global evangelization. In the book's closing chapters, Doddridge exhorts his readers to fervently desire the extension of God's reign and the conversion of the lost among the nations, and "to act in subordination to this great scheme of divine Providence, according to your abilities in their utmost extent."[15] This call to consider global mission was both startling and audacious, placing Doddridge well ahead of his time, as it would not be until some four decades later that such rhetoric became common in Nonconformist circles.

Doddridge began writing hymns during the early 1730s, most of which were put to immediate use in the worship of his Castle Hill congregation.[16] Many of his hymns were rooted in the biblical passages from which he preached, so that by the end of his life, his hymns spanned the entire corpus of the biblical canon. These hymns formed such a comprehensive commentary on Scripture that, upon their publication, they were arranged not by title or by topic, but by the order in which they corresponded to the biblical canon, stretching from Genesis to Revelation. Their content was so rich that several Nonconformist leaders recommended using Doddridge's hymns not only for singing but also as a poetic biblical commentary for private devotions and ministerial studies.[17]

In 1734, several other ministers and teachers began to assist Doddridge in his Northampton academy, among whom was Job Orton, who would become a lifelong friend, protégé, and fellow minister at Castle Hill, as well as his main biographer. While most of Doddridge's hymns saw only local and regional use during his lifetime,

---

14 Bishop, *Isaac Watts*, xvii; cf. Deacon, *Philip Doddridge*, 104–5.

15 Doddridge, *Rise and Progress*, 254.

16 Payne, *Eighteenth Century English Congregationalism*, 292.

17 See Humphreys, *Scriptural Hymns*, ix–x.

a few gained enough popularity to be included in one of the first compilation hymnals, produced in Scotland in 1745.[18]

After a bout of illness, Doddridge was sent south to the warmer climate of Lisbon, Portugal, but he did not recover and died shortly after his arrival there in 1751. In the weeks of his final decline, Doddridge left instructions for Orton to collect his hymns and make them more widely available, resulting in the publication of most of his hymns in the posthumous volume of 1755, *Hymns Founded on Various Texts*. Historical records make clear, however, that many of his hymns had already begun circulating in manuscript form well before that time, reaching farther beyond his own Northampton circle.[19]

Doddridge's poetic gifts were not as evident as those of Watts, but many of his hymns came into wide use because of Doddridge's stature among his contemporaries. Almost immediately upon its 1755 publication, Doddridge's *Hymns Founded on Various Texts* was regarded as a standard volume of Nonconformist hymnody, second only to Watts's *Hymns and Spiritual Songs* and *Psalms of David Imitated* (which were often published together in a single collection by this time). Thus, while only a small handful of Doddridge's hymns have been retained in modern worship—like "O Happy Day" and "Hark, the Glad Sound"—the impact of his hymns on eighteenth-century English worship should not be underestimated.

Missiological Influences in the Life of Philp Doddridge

Like Watts, Philip Doddridge came under the influence of the negative sensibilities within Nonconformism regarding the propriety and practicality of missionary endeavors. At the time, most of these ideas weighed against the prospect of global mission rather than for it. Global evangelization, when it was considered at all, was seen as a matter better left to the providence of God and as an inadvisable goal, given the evident spiritual needs of the Nonconformists' immediate

18 See Grant, *Translations and Paraphrases*.

19 Rivers and Wykes, *Dissenting Praise*, 70, 75.

surroundings. Doddridge, however, grew up a generation later than Watts, so the impact of the Evangelical Revival and the mission work of the Moravians had a greater influence on him.

Doddridge maintained correspondence with Protestant leaders across Europe and North America, including with pastors in New England and with Count Zinzendorf of the Moravians. This put him in a position to learn about the latest developments of the missionary activities of the American Congregationalists among the Native Americans and the Moravians in the Caribbean.[20] In the case of Zinzendorf, however, Doddridge grew rather less enchanted with him and the Moravian movement over time. He began to harbor suspicions regarding the enthusiasm they accorded to certain doctrinal emphases, a concern shared by many English Christians. These doubts also extended to the revivalists, touching on some of the emotionally driven methods the Methodists used in their outreach. In a 1743 letter, Doddridge wrote, "I had, indeed, great expectations from the Methodists and Moravians. I am grieved from my very heart, that so many things have occurred among them which have been quite unjustifiable."[21]

Doddridge's relationship with New England pastors remained positive, but his support of their labors was not widely shared among his colleagues. While Doddridge, like Watts, had been a regular correspondent with New England revivalists, their advocacy for North America's "Great Awakening" was not always well-received in Britain, where a significant majority of their fellow Nonconformists were suspicious of both the methods and the results associated with the movement.[22]

Nonetheless, the work of Massachusetts pastor Jonathan Edwards significantly impacted Doddridge's thought. In two important ways, Edwards prompted Doddridge to consider world evangelization,

---

20 Strivens, *Philip Doddridge*, 145–46; cf. Van den Berg and Nuttall, *Philip Doddridge*, 11.

21 Quoted in Harris, "Philip Doddridge," 255; see also Orton, *Memoirs*, 177.

22 O'Brien, "Transatlantic Community," 816.

entertaining ideas that, in large part, had not yet crossed the minds of his Nonconformist colleagues. It was Edwards's publication of David Brainerd's mission journals among the Native Americans that showed Doddridge the possibilities of cross-cultural ministry, and Doddridge was also deeply touched by Edwards's vision for a concerted effort by Christians to devote themselves to prayer for global revival.[23]

At the same time that these missional influences were rising across the Atlantic, conditions in England were starting to shift. By Doddridge's day, the memories of the worst repressions against Nonconformists were beginning to fade. There had been some flare-ups of anti-Dissenting sentiment in the decades following the Act of Toleration in 1689—most significantly from 1710 to 1714, during Watts's ministry—and while certain social restrictions remained upon Nonconformists, their place in English society had become a fact of life, so state-sponsored persecution was largely a thing of the past. By the end of the 1730s, the situation had changed enough that they were able to campaign for progressive changes in church-state relations without fear of reprisal.[24]

In this new milieu, Nonconformist attention began to move away from an inward-focused and defensive mentality, and toward a more outward-focused mindset, which would in time become more congenial to both revivalism and mission.[25] Fewer Nonconformist publications focused on doctrinal polemics against Anglicanism, instead placing their attention on questions relating to other theological and ecclesiological concerns. Doddridge even made some tentative steps toward reestablishing communion between the Anglican church and the Nonconformists (which was an occasional hope of Presbyterians, but not usually of Congregationalists).[26]

---

23 See Kidd, *Protestant Interest*, 171–72.

24 See Maclear, "Isaac Watts," 30–31; cf. Seed, *Dissenting Histories*, 22.

25 Crawford, "Origins," 373; see also Nuttall, "Methodism and the Older Dissent," 259–74.

26 Carter, "Philip Doddridge," 30; see also Seed, *Dissenting Histories*, 14; Harris, "Philip Doddridge," 262–64; Payne, "Eighteenth Century English Congregationalism," 297–98.

Doddridge was also involved in the theological debates that helped ignite some of the new missiological ideas forming within Nonconformism. One such debate was particular to the Calvinist circles in which Doddridge worked: the question of how unregenerated people should be addressed with the gospel. The way this question was usually framed (referred to at the time as the "modern question") was whether it was the duty of unconverted sinners, upon hearing the gospel, to believe in God.[27] While this question of duty might seem a somewhat obscure matter, it was central to the practices that flowed from it. To decide, as Doddridge did, that it *was* the duty of unconverted sinners to respond in faith to the gospel also meant that the preachers and missionaries presenting that gospel should employ methods of direct address, with all their powers of appeal, to call sinners toward such a response. The opposing position, holding a stricter Calvinist stance, viewed the calling of sinners as entirely a matter for the providence of God, asserting that those who were elect would respond to the gospel regardless of how they encountered it.

This theological question helped to focus attention on individual sinners and the means by which they encountered the gospel, rather than solely on the electing work of God. While both positions ascribed the work of God's grace in electing people as the definitive element of whether they would respond to the gospel, those on Doddridge's side argued that God ordains not only the outcome of the gospel's proclamation but the means as well. This position thus brought the methods of evangelism and their effectiveness in reaching nonbelievers into sharper focus. The debate over the "modern question" was part of a growing appreciation in eighteenth-century Calvinist circles that the doctrine of God's sovereignty did not preclude human action and intentionality.[28] The "modern question" would loom large in the story of Nonconformist

27 Strivens, *Philip Doddridge*, 142.

28 Bosch, *Transforming Mission*, 292.

missiology, as it re-emerged in the 1780s and sparked Andrew Fuller's influential perspective on the relationship between Calvinism and Nonconformist missions.[29]

For Doddridge, the question of foreign missions was an issue he considered and promoted, rather than heard about with interest, as did Watts. A half-century before William Carey sparked a revolution by proposing the formation of a foreign mission society, Doddridge had floated the same idea. In 1741, Doddridge addressed a meeting of clergymen in the town of Denton and offered an address titled "Some Hints of a Scheme…for the Revival of Religion in our Parts." His scheme included ten main points, all focused on ways to encourage the growth of the local church and the piety of its congregants. Doddridge had been inclined to add a further point and would have done so had he not felt the sermon was growing too long. This eleventh point ended up going unpresented at Denton, but it was published in his preface to the address when it was released in pamphlet form. The eleventh point of his program was "that something might be done among the dissenting churches, towards the propagation of Christianity abroad."[30] While Doddridge did not actually create a mission society, he was one of the first voices in English Nonconformism to promote the idea. Referring to Doddridge's scheme at Denton, historian Ernest Payne later wrote, "had its explicit pleas been acted on, [it] would have given to Congregational ministers the honour, which came to a company of Baptists fifty years later . . . of starting the first modern missionary society."[31]

Near the end of his life, Doddridge was quoted as saying, "I am now intent upon having something done among the Dissenters in a more public manner for propagating the Gospel abroad, which lies near to my heart."[32] Such a suggestion was momentous for its time,

---

29 Nuttall, "Northamptonshire and *The Modern Question*," 101–2.

30 Orton, *Memoirs*, 176.

31 Payne, "Eighteenth Century English Congregationalism," 296; see also Nuttall, *Philip Doddridge*, 87–93.

32 Carter, "Philip Doddridge," 32.

and while he never saw such efforts come to fruition, he planted the seeds of a later harvest in the outlook of his hymns. His stance was unashamedly outward, giving special attention to social concerns that extended both to the proclamation of the gospel and to works of mercy. With his focus on the call of the Christian conscience to help the outcast and the unsaved, the nations which lay beyond the reach of the gospel's spread could not long escape Doddridge's notice.

Philip Doddridge's Hymns

Just as the hymn-writing career of Isaac Watts was drawing to a close, the hymns of Philip Doddridge began to be put to use. Doddridge was nearly a generation younger than Watts, though their ministry careers overlapped, and Doddridge himself served as one of Watts's first biographers. Inspired by Watts's example, Doddridge made it his practice to compose new hymns for his congregation, usually based on the same biblical text as his sermon for the week.

His posthumous collection, *Hymns Founded on Various Texts*, is divided into two parts: the first consists of hymns directly derived from or inspired by biblical passages, arranged in order from Genesis to Revelation, and the second contains hymns devoted to specific occasions and settings in the Christian life. In some printings, these two sections were presented as separate works: *Hymns and Spiritual Songs* and *Hymns on Particular Occasions*. Doddridge's scriptural hymns were so thorough in their presentation of biblical themes—encompassing the entire canon—that one later editor wrote, "they constitute a very complete system of 'Bible Divinity' . . . extending from the first book of the Sacred Records to the last."[33]

While Doddridge's hymns lacked some of the literary beauty that Watts achieved, he was fully Watts's equal as a theologian and an expositor of Scripture, and his hymns exude a warmth of spirit that won them a lasting place in English hymnody. One nineteenth-century historian put it this way: "[Doddridge] had not the same poetic genius

33 Humphreys, *Scriptural Hymns*, ix.

with which his friend Isaac Watts was endowed . . . but there is a sweetness and tenderness in Doddridge's versifications on devotional subjects, in admirable harmony with his amiable character."[34] Not as many of his hymns became part of the popular Christian repertoire as did Watts's, but he was widely appreciated, and his work, alongside Watts, often formed the core of the earliest compilation hymnals in the late eighteenth century.

What makes Doddridge's hymns particularly significant for our purposes is that they represent another step in the growth of missional awareness in Nonconformist worship. Unlike Watts, who seems to have stumbled unintentionally into writing the profoundly missional hymns of his *Psalms of David Imitated,* we know from Doddridge's other works that his infusion of missiological reflection was calculated and intentional. With the exception of the anomalously high levels of missiological content in *Psalms of David Imitated,* Doddridge's hymns stand head and shoulders above all his contemporaries in terms of the frequency with which he called on such themes. Missiological ideas are almost nowhere present in any of the other Nonconformist hymnographers between Watts and himself, but they appear regularly in Doddridge's hymns.

To see how Doddridge's missional content is more intentional than Watts's, consider the following example from *Hymns Founded on Various Texts*:

> Behold our God, he owns his name;
> Jehovah all our songs proclaim
> With shouts of wonder and of joy:
> Long have we waited for his grace,
> No longer now his love delays
> For Zion his own arm to employ.

34 Stoughton, *Religion in England,* 343.

We charge our souls the joy to feel:
We charge our tongues his praise to tell:
The Almighty Saviour! This is he!
He pours his streams of grace abroad,
Till all the Earth confess [him] God,
And lands remote his glory see.[35]

These are the first two verses of a longer hymn, inspired by Isaiah 25:6–9. Unlike Watts, Doddridge didn't usually write paraphrases (or, in Watts's terminology, "imitations") of biblical passages. Rather, like the preacher that he was, Doddridge wrote hymns that were expositional—rooted in a particular text but, like a sermon, expanding on it with further reflections and applications.

In this case, the active intentionality of the call leaps off the page. Not only does Doddridge reference a vision of the whole world coming to know the glory of God, but he also adds a note of personal, collective duty and responsibility that one must search for vainly in Watts: "We charge our tongues his praise to tell." A skeptic might note, however, that this "charge" is made only in the context of God's praise, and perhaps not of evangelistic activity, especially since the reference to the nations coming to know God is attributed to God's own action: "*He* pours his streams of grace abroad." But an example from another hymn, inspired by Acts 17:23, shows that Doddridge certainly had a sense of English Christianity's duty toward the nations:

Thou, mighty Lord, art God alone,
A King of majesty unknown;
And all thy dazzling glories rise
Beyond the reach of angels' eyes.

Yet through this Earth thy works proclaim
Some notice of thy reverend name;
And, where the gracious Gospel shines,
We read it in the fairest lines.

35 Doddridge, *Hymns*, 76.

But O! how few of Adam's race
Have learned thy nature and thy ways!
While thousands, even in the lands of light,
Are buried in Egyptian night.

They tread thy courts, thy Word they hear,
And to thy solemn rites draw near;
Yet, though salvation seems so nigh,
Because they know not God, they die.

Send thy victorious Gospel forth
Wide from these regions of the north;
And through thy churches grace impart
To write thy name on every heart.[36]

In this hymn, Doddridge laments the fact that so many people, all across the globe, do not yet know God (including, it seems, the Catholic populations of continental Europe). In the final stanza, he expresses a statement that was radical for its time: a plea for God to use his own area, his own communion of churches, to accomplish the evangelization of the world. The responsibility entailed here is clear: He prays that the gospel would spread "wide from these regions of the north" (i.e., Britain and other traditionally Protestant areas). The closing line of that stanza can even be read as an invitation for God to impart the grace that will motivate those Christians "to write thy name on every heart." While God is still identified as the active agent in this process (as one would expect from a Calvinist hymnographer), there is clearly an elevated sense of personal and collective responsibility for world mission in this hymn.

Note also that Doddridge includes an element of emotional fervor in his vision of global mission, a tenor that was lacking in Watts's treatment of the subject. While Watts offered prophetic scenes of joy at the prospect of all nations praising God, one senses in Doddridge's hymns a yearning, a broken-hearted longing for the

36 Doddridge, 221–22.

salvation of the nations. This same sense can be seen in another of Doddridge's hymns (of which selected stanzas appear below), this one inspired by Isaiah 66:8:

> Behold with pleasing ecstasy
> The Gospel-standard lifted high,
> That all the nations from afar
> May in the great salvation share.
>
> Why then, Almighty Saviour, why
> Do wretched souls in millions die?
> While wide the infernal tyrant reigns
> O'er spacious realms in ponderous chains.
>
> And shall he still go on to boast,
> The cross its energy hath lost?
> And shall thy servants still complain,
> Their labours, and their tears are vain?
>
> Awake, all conquering arm, awake,
> And hell's extensive empire shake;
> Assert the honours of thy throne,
> And call this ruined world thine own.
>
> Scarce can our glowing hearts endure
> A world where thou art known no more;
> Transform it, Lord, by conquering love,
> Or bear us to the realms above.[37]

There is a heart-wrenching tone to this hymn; one senses the passion and fervency with which Doddridge desires to see the salvation of the nations. Readers should be able to notice, too, the much greater clarity with which the vision of global mission is expressed compared to the hymns of Isaac Watts. While Watts's *Psalms of David Imitated* contain a higher frequency of missional content than Doddridge's collection (largely due to the underlying missiology of the biblical psalms), Doddridge's

37 Doddridge, 107–8.

expression of that content is much closer to the clarity and intentionality of the call that William Carey would issue a half-century later.

The only thing lacking from Doddridge's vision, it seems, was the actual organization and implementation of a mission society. He foresaw that step—even wrote about it in his published address from the Denton meeting—but did not undertake the logistics to bring it about. It may have been that his Nonconformist circle was still not ready for it. Indeed, for all of Doddridge's missional vision, he is something of a man alone in the mid-century English church. There were forces in motion for revival, for the evangelization of English society and of Britain's colonists in far-flung areas, but the idea of actively sending out missionaries in cross-cultural, border-spanning enterprises was not yet on any other Englishman's horizon. And while there were outside influences already leaning in that direction—think again of the Moravians—Doddridge's Calvinist circles remained caught in the thick of theological debates that too often seemed content to leave the conversion of the nations to the work of God alone. Even when Carey began casting his vision in Reformed-Nonconformist circles fifty years later, he still encountered the same hesitations.

What was needed in Doddridge's day, then, was not the radical step of a mission society, which likely would have failed due to insufficient support. No, what was needed was a way to help people see beyond their narrow provincial and theological horizons, to catch some of the biblical vision for the salvation of the whole world, and to gain a sense of the part they could play in that story. The hymns of Philip Doddridge, together with Watts's *Psalms of David Imitated*, fit that need. By singing hymns like the ones above, a grander missional vision was worked like leaven into the dough of Nonconformist church life. Week by week and year by year, that vision grew, gradually internalized in tens of thousands of hearts and minds across England and North America. And then, a half-century later, the time was finally right. Their hearts, like Doddridge's, had come to yearn for the salvation of the nations.

7

Proclaim His Grace Abroad

The Ongoing Intertwining of Mission and Hymn

At this point, we need to take a look at what actually happened in Nonconformist churches between the introduction of these hymns and the launch of the mission movement. What kind of fruit did the hymns bear in the life of the church? Where can we see their influence?

If the premise is that the inspiration for the launch of the Protestant mission movement of the 1790s came in part from the hymns introduced more than a half-century earlier, the best source for demonstrating that connection is the one that actually ignited the movement in 1792: William Carey's *Enquiry*. So far, we've merely pointed out elements of hymns that sound plausibly missional to our ears, but the question remains whether they actually align with the missional sensibilities that emerged in the 1790s. To establish a connection between the hymns of the time and the missiology of the time, we must ask: Are the themes we see in the hymns the same ones that appear in Carey's *Enquiry*, the touchstone missiological treatise of its age?

Missiological Themes Connecting Earlier Hymns to William Carey

In the dissertation research underlying this book, a literary survey was undertaken in which Carey's *Enquiry* was "coded" for all the missiological themes that appear in its pages, and then the corpus of earlier hymns was studied for the appearance of those coded themes. (This research methodology is known as qualitative content analysis.) In this way, the research could reveal the introduction and development of those themes in early Nonconformist hymns, the same themes Carey would later use to build his case for world mission. Before we discuss the results of those datasets, it's worth providing a brief synopsis of Nonconformist thought in the second half of the eighteenth century to illustrate the continued growth of the missional mindset that Carey's work exemplifies.

The experience of Nonconformist Christians had begun to shift by this time. The persecutions of the late 1600s were now far behind them, receding beyond memory, and even the social stigma against them was lightening.[1] Congregationalists and Baptists were still groups on the margins, but through their sheer persistence, their status was now more accepted in British life, and so their situation had gradually grown more secure. As the fear of persecution began to lift, their focus began to change, shifting from an insular emphasis on the apologetic defense of their doctrinal distinctives to a more outward-facing interest.[2]

This transition from an inward-facing movement to an outward-facing one was also aided by some of the factors outlined in chapter 2. The zeal and excitement of the Evangelical Revival had begun to trickle into English Nonconformist churches, despite their earlier suspicions about the "enthusiasm" the revival produced. This was especially assisted by the fact that the North American side of that revival, called the Great Awakening, had prominent Congregationalists among its leaders.

The work of the Massachusetts pastor Jonathan Edwards was of particular interest to English Nonconformists, and both Watts and Doddridge played a role in popularizing his books back in the

1 See Maclear, "Isaac Watts," 30–31.

2 Crawford, "Origins," 373; see also Nuttall, "Methodism and the Older Dissent," 259–74.

mother country. Edwards, the famous preacher of "Sinners in the Hands of an Angry God" and the author of *Religious Affections*, was a kindred spirit to his contemporary Philip Doddridge when it came to global missions. While Doddridge was contemplating ways to launch mission societies in England and writing missiological themes into his hymns, Edwards was dreaming of the evangelization of the world, encouraging a program of concerted prayer toward that end.[3] Edwards was also the man behind the publication of David Brainerd's journals, which popularized the example of the intrepid young missionary. There was a great deal of cross-pollination between the English and American branches of the Nonconformist churches, and while one can see Edwards's missional thinking flowing from west to east, it is worth noting that the mission-rich hymns of Watts's *Psalms of David Imitated* had already made the crossing in the other direction and had been regularly used in North American contexts, including in Brainerd's own ministry.[4]

These influences from the 1730s and '40s—the Evangelical Revival and the work of North American missionaries—certainly had a shaping influence on English Nonconformism, but it took a long while for those effects to be felt across the entire movement. Efforts to pray for the salvation of the nations sprang up sporadically, but they were much more the exception than the rule.

Truth be told, a sense of the scope of global missions was still, at best, nascent and undefined in most people's minds. The mid-1700s were relatively early in the British Empire's colonial expansion—still more than a century removed from the height of its reach in the late nineteenth and early twentieth centuries. Most people's perspectives were still limited by a narrow geographic horizon, and while the existence of "heathen" nations beyond that circle was acknowledged, it was still difficult to feel love or pity for the vague entities that

3 See Kidd, *Protestant Interest*, 171–72.

4 Milner, *Life, Times, and Correspondence*, 539; Doddridge, *Abridgement*, 74; Bond *Poetic Wonder*, 68; King, "Psalms," 41–42.

existed beyond the shadowy borders of the known world. One of the events that began to shift this trend in English society was the publication of Captain James Cook's explorations in the 1770s, which highlighted the true scale of the task: the sheer, unimagined number of places and people groups that were still out there, as yet untouched by Christian influence.[5]

It was not until the 1780s that one could trace a significant increase in the Nonconformist resolve to engage in world missions. While their interest in mission had been gradually growing since the early decades of the century, there had not been a correlating sense of responsibility or intentionality, except in rare cases like Edwards and Doddridge. However, once we reached the 1780s, the forces that had been percolating under the surface for decades suddenly began to emerge into the light. Theologians like Andrew Fuller began preaching on the necessity of world mission, and pastors' groups began considering the subject together.[6] Even the Methodists—at this time still more focused on local evangelism than global mission, a hesitancy partly due to their growing distance from Moravian influence—had leaders producing early forms of missiological treatises. Most notable in this regard is Thomas Coke, who wrote a plan for a Methodist missionary society in 1783, but his vision did not come to fruition until 1813, two decades after the Nonconformist missionary societies were launched.[7]

Despite the rise in interest and intentionality in the 1780s, there was still significant resistance to the idea in some Nonconformist circles. Strong forms of Calvinist doctrine did not logically exclude evangelism or mission, but historically speaking, they did have the effect of dampening some of the impetus for missional thinking. Calvinist doctrine, considered as such, did not restrict mission from

5 Walker, *History of the Christian Church*, 471; cf. Beeching, *Open Path*, 86.

6 Chute, Finn, and Haykin, *Baptist Story*, 102–5.

7 See Stanley, *History of the Baptist Missionary Society*, 2; Klauber and Manetsch, *Great Commission*, 46.

developing—in the nineteenth century, much of the global expansion of Protestant Christianity would come from Calvinist-influenced traditions—but in the eighteenth century, some debates about divine providence and human action resulted in a certain inertia against the development of missiological thought.[8]

Consider again, for example, Isaac Watts's reaction to hearing word of the revivals breaking out in New England in the late 1730s:

> These [revivals] are certainly little specimens of what Christ and his grace can do when he shall begin to revive his own work and to spread his Kingdom thro' the earth . . . I adore his good pleasure and rejoice, but wait for the blessing in European countries.[9]

In this quote, Watts indicates that he expects the spread of Christianity in the world to come primarily through Christ's future action, for which the proper response is to wait. There is no assumption detectable here that promoting circumstances in which revival might flourish or carrying out missionary activities might themselves be the actions through which Christ accomplishes his plan. Watts's reaction fit with a general sense among Reformed Nonconformists that God's eschatological plan for the world included a final, global revival, but that it would come in God's own timing.[10]

Similarly, the implicit drag of strong Calvinist conceptions is evident in a famous anecdote from the ministry of William Carey near the end of the eighteenth century. Accounts vary, but the story goes that during Carey's early ministry, before the publication of his missionary treatise, he was rebuffed by a senior clergyman when he suggested that the missionary mandate given to Jesus's disciples might also apply to later generations of Christians. "Young man, sit

8 Lambert, *Inventing the "Great Awakening,"* 26–28; Crawford, "Origins," 373; see also Bosch, *Transforming Mission*, 263.

9 Quoted in Kidd, *Great Awakening*, 21.

10 Klauber and Manetsch, *Great Commission*, 89–92.

down," the other cleric, John Ryland, Sr., is recorded as saying. "When God pleases to convert the heathen, He'll do it without consulting you or me."[11]

Ryland's famous quote is sometimes taken as an expression of hyper-Calvinism, holding to the belief that God's sovereignty is so completely expressed in his electing grace that there is no real place for human agency in the work of saving nonbelievers. Some scholars have argued, however, that Ryland's response may not reflect an emphasis on God's electing grace, but rather on another commonly held Reformed position of the time, which subscribed to an eschatological view in which the conversion of non-Christian nations would occur in an end-of-the-age outpouring of the Holy Spirit, somewhat in the same manner as at Pentecost. If this is the case, then Ryland was telling Carey not to get ahead of God's sovereign plan for world history.[12] Either way, though, it comes back to a view of God's sovereign providence, either with regard to individual salvation or to God's plan for Christianity's progress in the world.

Carey persisted in the face of these doubts, publishing his 1792 treatise, *An Enquiry into the Obligation of Christians to Use Means for the Conversion of the Heathens*, whose title implies that there was still some opposition to the idea that Christians had a duty toward intentional engagement in missions. The very fact that he had to make the argument at all shows how persistent the resistance to the notion of world mission was. Nevertheless, once he had published his book, events moved rapidly. Despite lingering doubts among some thinkers, it was clear that Carey had tapped into a rising groundswell of support that was ready for action. Later in the same year, Carey's Baptists founded the first modern missionary society, and just three years later, the Congregationalists oversaw the launch of another such society.[13]

11 George, *Faithful Witness*, 53.

12 See Klauber and Manetsch, *Great Commission*, 89–92.

13 Stanley, *History of the Baptist Missionary Society*, 8; see also Walls, *Cross-Cultural Process*, 16–17.

The shape of Carey's argument in his *Enquiry* followed major lines of evidence from Scripture, church history, and global demographics. He made a theological case for global mission based on biblical references, particularly drawing on the Great Commission. He also pointed out the long legacy of missionary labors throughout church history, of which he and his fellow Englishmen were heirs, and he drew attention to the contemporary work of groups like the Moravians. His plea then turned to the needs of the world around them, drawing together demographic statistics for the known world and the availability of the gospel in various regions. By a sheer avalanche of numbers, he drove home his point to his readers: The vast majority of the world, numbering untold millions of people, still had little access to the gospel of Jesus Christ.

As Carey developed a comprehensive theological argument for world mission, he explored a number of different missiological themes. The table below presents those themes as they were coded for content analysis. These themes, extracted from Carey's *Enquiry*, formed the basis for researching the development of missiological themes in earlier hymns: Did the hymns of Watts convey the same ideas as Carey's treatise, despite being separated by three-quarters of a century? In large part, as the evidence will show, they did (though not always in the most proactive sense).

Missiological Themes in William Carey's *Enquiry*

Theme 1(A): The doctrine of divine lordship over the whole world

Theme 1(B): The expansion of divine lordship to the whole world

Theme 1(C): The worldwide spread of submission to divine lordship, as effected by the intentional actions of Christians

Theme 2(A): The necessity (and/or inequal distribution) of knowledge of the gospel

Theme 2(B): The growth of the knowledge of the gospel

Theme 2(C): The spread of knowledge of the gospel through the intentional actions of Christians

Theme 3(A): Expressions of prayer for the nations

Theme 3(B): The Christian obligation to pray for the nations

Theme 4: The practice of going (or being sent out)

Theme 5: Missionary activity as obedience to biblical commands

Theme 6: Missionary activity as spiritual warfare

Theme 7: Missionary activity as a work of faith

Theme 8(A): General awareness of the division between Christian and "heathen" areas of the world

Theme 8(B): Emphasis on specific geographical areas, people groups, and/or their needs

Theme 9: Positive effects of the gospel on the nations

Theme 10: Awareness of historical mission movements

Theme 11: Awareness of their opportunity for mission in their present historical moment

Theme 12: The spiritual state of non-Christians as a subject of emotional concern

These are all themes that one might expect to find in a missiological treatise, like Carey's *Enquiry*. They are not, however, themes that one would expect to find in a hymn unless that hymn is specifically written with global missions in mind. Most modern hymns, even after the advent of the Protestant mission movement, would not rank particularly high in the usage of these themes, with the major exception of the later genre of "mission hymns." So, in looking back at the earliest hymns of the eighteenth century, before the mission movement began, one would not expect to find a lot of these missiological themes.

In fact, among all the other hymn-writers besides Isaac Watts, that expectation would be proved right. The early hymns of Nonconformist figures like Benjamin Keach, Joseph Stennett, and Simeon Browne—

all contemporaries of Watts—show a vanishingly small presence of missiological themes. The average statistical rate for the appearance of any of the themes above was found to be only about 0.3 percent, and those appearances were all judged to be weakly present (meaning that they showed no real missional sensibility but only appeared as afterthoughts to other doctrines highlighted in the hymns). To present the results more clearly, only one hymn in the entire corpus of works by the other hymnographers was found to contain significant missiological content: one of Joseph Stennett's hymns, which repeated the Great Commission text almost word for word. In the case of that hymn, however, the main point wasn't even mission at all; the hymn was more interested in Christ's institution of baptism (selected stanzas are given here):

> The sacred Body of our Lord,
> Which on the cross had bled,
> Three days lay buried in the grave,
> And then rose from the dead.
>
> His presence the desponding hearts
> Of his disciples cheers:
> His voice they hear, his scars survey,
> Which banish doubts and fears.
>
> For thus the Mediator spoke,
> "All Power in Earth and Heav'n
> To Me, triumphant o'er the grave,
> Is by my Father given.
>
> "Go therefore teach the nations all
> What you have learned of Me;
> Baptize them in the awful Name
> Of the eternal Three.
>
> "Teach them whatever I command;
> My presence I assure,
> To crown your labours with success,
> While Heaven and Earth endure."

Lord! we thy wondrous grace adore,
Thy awful Word revere;
Thy death and thy revival both
Our baptism makes appear.[14]

Note that while Stennett faithfully repeats the rich missiological content of the Great Commission, the hymn indicates that Jesus's original disciples are the recipients of that charge. When Stennett mentions an application for his own contemporary audience, it is baptism, not mission, that he emphasizes. Essentially, then, the available evidence from the hymns confirms the overall picture of eighteenth-century Nonconformism that we can glean from other sources: it was a Christian community without any real sense of a global missionary mandate.

That's the picture from all the other sources. Watts, however, was an outlier, and a peculiar one at that. While most of his hymns were not overtly missiological, *Hymns and Spiritual Songs* (his first major hymnbook) still showed a threefold increase in missiological content over the baseline level in other sources. That might sound significant, but in reality, we're still talking about a statistical rate of appearance of less than one percent. Watts's early missiological themes pop up most frequently regarding the sovereignty of God over the whole world—an idea that is foundational for further missiological reflection, but which doesn't yet indicate a fully formed missional sensibility, at least not on its own.

The big jump, as readers should now expect, came with Watts's 1719 publication of his *Psalms of David Imitated*. Here, the rate of appearance of missiological themes shows a tenfold increase compared to other Nonconformist hymnographers of the same period. This brings Watts's *Psalms of David Imitated* into the same statistical range as modern hymnals that contain whole sections devoted to hymns of mission and evangelism. For its own time, though, it appears wildly

14 Stennett, *Hymns Compos'd*, 4–5.

out of place. Even Doddridge's hymnbook does not contain the same rate of missiological themes, though Doddridge had a more developed missional awareness than Watts.

In the content analysis research sessions, coders considered not only the appearance of missiological themes within the whole corpus of hymns but also the question of how many hymns, considered as full pieces, appeared to be substantially missional in focus. It is possible, for example, for a hymn to reference a missiological theme—like the lordship of Christ over all nations—in a tangential manner while the full hymn is not really about mission at all. (That sort of occurrence accounts for the majority of the thematic dataset in most sources.) By counting the number of "mission hymns" separately from the raw data of a line-by-line thematic tally, it provided another way of tallying the results, and the numbers in this hymn-tally dataset confirmed the general spread of the thematic dataset. Minor Nonconformist sources showed an average rate of mission-oriented hymns at 0.5 percent or less (depending on whether they were Baptist or Congregational sources), a rate that is probably statistically irrelevant. Watts's early sources (all except his *Psalms of David Imitated*) were higher, close to one percent, largely on the strength of paraphrase hymns drawn straight from Scripture. Doddridge's hymnal was a good deal stronger yet, showing a rate of mission-oriented hymns at 2.1 percent, which falls within the same range as most modern hymnals (often two to four percent). But Watts's *Psalms of David Imitated* again stands apart from the rest by a significant measure, at 3.5 percent—which would again place his book among the most mission-oriented hymnals today.

As argued in chapter 5, the uniqueness of Watts's contributions in the *Psalms of David Imitated* is striking. But it's also worth reminding ourselves that Watts seldom expresses his missiological themes in the most active sense. Missiological themes present throughout the hymns, but one element they lack is a motivating sense of duty. Despite the richness of mission hymns like "Jesus Shall Reign" or the global vision of "Joy to the World," Watts's hymns almost never take the corollary step of saying, "Yes, the nations belong to Christ and need to hear his gospel, *and therefore we should take it to them.*"

This is where Doddridge, coming a generation after Watts, represents a new and powerful development of missional thinking in the Nonconformist churches. Doddridge's hymns are more missional than all of Watts's non-*Psalms* hymns by a fair measure, and while they don't match the sheer statistical frequency of missiological themes in the *Psalms of David Imitated,* Doddridge's use of those themes is more pointed, direct, and self-aware regarding the Christian duty toward evangelism. As the previous chapter indicated, Doddridge's hymns directly express the idea that English Christians—even the very singers of the hymns themselves—have a necessary role in making the gospel known to the nations.

With regard to the missiological themes in the table above, this means that Watts was using a lot of the simpler, more straightforward ones—often the divided themes marked with an "A"—while Doddridge was using more developed themes, like those marked with a "B" or "C." Together, these two major Nonconformist hymnographers show that, while there certainly was a long arc of development in their use of missiological themes, they were indeed employing most of the same ideas that Carey would later draw from. Of the coded themes from Carey's *Enquiry,* all but two showed repeated appearances in earlier Nonconformist hymns, and several clusters of the most important themes were richly interwoven throughout Watts's and Doddridge's contributions.

We have noted in the preceding chapters that the missional sensibilities expressed in Watts's *Psalms of David Imitated* and in the hymns of Philip Doddridge were unique, to the point of being out of place for their time. In the case of the *Psalms of David Imitated,* the hymns reflect a level of missiological engagement even higher than the author's own thought. For Doddridge, his missional awareness was more conscious and intentional than Watts's, more pronounced than almost any other of his Nonconformist contemporaries.

So in noting that these two hymnographers were using the same missiological themes that Carey used to launch the mission movement at the end of the century, we are not suggesting that these hymns reflect a profound missional awareness that was already present in Nonconformist churches. Rather, we are suggesting that the hymns themselves became the vehicle for the growth of that awareness. This is the conclusion at which the research arrived: *the hymns of Watts and Doddridge represented an independent infusion of missiological thought into Nonconformist life, and the regular use of that thought in congregational singing exercised a shaping influence on the Nonconformist mindset as a whole.* While there are many other historical causes that led to the launch of the Protestant mission movement, the rise of missiologically rich hymns early in the eighteenth century appears to be another such cause—one that has largely gone unnoticed until now.

This conclusion gains an added layer of plausibility when one considers the power of hymnody as a medium of communication. Congregational song is almost ideally suited for the long, slow work of shaping theological sensibilities. By taking a theologically rich text, setting it to music, singing it in a participatory way, and repeating that activity at regular intervals, the messages within hymns tend to work their way into the worshipers' conception of the Christian life. A sermon can be an effective tool in its proper context, and a book can have a broad and significant effect, but there is almost nothing like the power of song to mold the underlying values and sentiments of an entire population toward a new sense of missional awareness.

The Continuing Legacy of Hymns in the Eighteenth Century

The initial wave of Nonconformist hymnody began (on a small scale) with the Baptists of the 1690s and became a tidal wave through the work of Isaac Watts. That surge was then reinforced by Doddridge's later contributions, who not only added his own hymns but also helped further popularize Watts's. This wave did not die out with the passing of Watts and Doddridge in the mid-1700s but expanded. New hymnwriters emerged in the mid-to-late eighteenth century.

The hymns that John and Charles Wesley wrote as part of the Evangelical Revival in the Anglican and Methodist communions gradually began to trickle into Nonconformist worship as well. These Wesleyan hymns, which even included some translated contributions from the Moravians, were not always as missiologically rich as Doddridge's hymns or those in the *Psalms of David Imitated*, but they carried overtones of passionate devotion and commitment to God's will.[15] As such, the songs of the Evangelical Revival complemented the new mission-hymns of the Nonconformist churches, reinforcing a sense of all-out consecration to God's work in one's life and in the world at large.

At the same time, new Nonconformist hymnographers arose, continuing the thematic contributions of Watts, Doddridge, and the early Baptists. One of the foremost of these was the British Baptist poet Anne Steele, whose hymns began to appear for public use in the 1760s. In Steele, we see the same intensity of private devotion that inspired several other Baptist hymnographers of the mid-1700s, like Daniel Turner and Benjamin Wallin, but now with an added sense of evangelical zeal. Much like Doddridge's hymns, Steele's reflections on one's personal relationship with Christ would overflow into zeal for the spread of the gospel. While this was not the foremost theme of her hymns, the fact that it appears at all—in contrast to most of her Baptist antecedents—shows the influence that the popular hymnography of Watts, Doddridge, and the Wesleys was beginning to have.

Like Watts, Steele wrote some hymns directly from the psalms, and the implicit missiology of the psalms comes to the forefront in her verses:

15 See Rack, "John Wesley," 37; Randall, "Missional Spirituality," 210–11.

Then shall my heart and tongue proclaim
The praises of my God,
My songs with grateful rapture flame,
And spread thy praise abroad.[16]

While Steele does not always evoke a sense of personal responsibility to the missionary call, she frequently includes heartfelt cries of welcome and invitation to those who are lost. Consider the final verse of her hymn "Ye Wretched, Starving Poor":

Ten thousand thousand more
Are welcome still to come;
Ye longing souls, the grace adore;
Approach, there yet is room.[17]

A similar sentiment can be found in her hymn "The Savior Calls, Let Every Ear":

O sinners, come, hear mercy's voice,
The gracious call obey;
Mercy invites you to heavenly joys,
And can you yet delay?[18]

In all these hymns, Steele shows that the pattern established in the work of Watts and Doddridge continues on, now also bearing marks of cross-pollination with the zeal of the Evangelical Revival. A few other minor hymnwriters emerged in Baptist and Congregationalist circles at the same time, and their works show similar thematic patterns. In the decade following Steele's work, the Golden Age of Hymns would rise to yet another summit of achievement, demonstrating that the fervent devotional passion of the revivals was still rising in hymns from other quarters. This can be seen in the evangelical-Anglican hymnbook that would eventually stand shoulder-to-shoulder with the prominence of Watts's earlier works: the 1779 *Olney Hymns*, by John

16 Steele, *Poems*, Vol. 2, 142.

17 Steele, Vol. 1, 17.

18 Steele, Vol. 1, 163.

Newton and William Cowper, which gave the world such classics as "Amazing Grace," "Glorious Things of Thee Are Spoken," and "How Sweet the Name of Jesus Sounds."

Within Nonconformist circles, however, there was still no rivaling Watts's domination of the church's hymnody, especially through his *Psalms of David Imitated.* As the decades passed, the hymns from his 1719 opus magnum were used more frequently, not less.[19] It often provided the perfect entry point for churches whose only exposure to congregational song had been the use of biblical psalms, for which Watts's *Psalms of David Imitated* offered an initial half-step toward the use of "men's composures" as part of the sung liturgy of the church. Once introduced into a congregation, even if it stirred up controversy, Watts's *Psalms of David Imitated* usually won over the laypeople fairly quickly, thanks to Watts's poetic mastery and devotional expressiveness.

The works of Watts and Doddridge began to exercise an even wider reach when, beginning in the late 1760s, the first major compilation hymnals were published. John Wesley had experimented with the idea a few decades earlier, but until about two-thirds of the way through the eighteenth century, most hymns were available only in single-author publications. The rise of compilation hymnals allowed congregations to utilize the most popular hymns, and in the earliest such Nonconformist hymnals, it was Watts and Doddridge whose work dominated the contributions.[20] So as the century progressed, approaching the 1780s and '90s—in which other events began to line up for the establishment of the first Baptist and Congregationalist mission agencies—Watts's *Psalms* and Doddridge's hymns were exercising an ever-expanding influence on the minds and hearts of both Baptists and Congregationalists.

---

19 See Benson, *English Hymn*, 1962, 123–24; Gillman, *Evolution of the English Hymn*, 207; Davie, *Gathered Church*, 33–34.

20 See Benson, *English Hymn*, 212.

Given this pattern, it should come as no surprise that when William Carey produced his missiological treatise in 1792, many of the themes he drew on were ones that had already appeared in the hymns of Watts and Doddridge. This is not to diminish William Carey's contributions, of course—he marshaled historical precedent and demographic data in his treatise to produce a compelling case for world mission in a way that no hymn ever could, and his book marked a turning point in the history of missions.

But when the context of Nonconformist hymnody is brought into the picture, Carey's contribution is seen in its proper light, like a jewel in its setting. His work constituted a pivotal turning point in the history of Christian mission, but rather than the seminal brainchild of an isolated genius, the *Enquiry* can now be seen as something even more compelling: the radical reformulation of an idea that the Holy Spirit had nurtured in the worship of Nonconformist churches over the course of nearly a century. The Protestant mission movement, when viewed through the lens of hymnody, is less the achievement of a few great actors and more the achievement of the whole church of God, which had been growing toward a missional view of the world through the praises they sang together.

8

Let His Name Be Sung

Mission and Song for the Twenty-First Century

The thesis of this book—that one of the major factors preparing the way for the Protestant mission movement of the late 1700s was a fresh surge in English hymnody—invites reflection. While it is certainly valuable in a historical sense, adding to our knowledge of how these movements in church history unfolded, it also encourages contemporary applications. If the sung worship of the church proved so essential to a major work of God in the eighteenth century, might it not be so again in the twenty-first?

For pastors, worship leaders, and liturgists, the worship revolution of the 1700s offers insightful lessons. For those interested in replicating its effects and using the power of song to build up a congregation's awareness of specific theological points or inspire action in the world, there are two things to consider. First, we must acknowledge the rich potential of songs as vehicles for theological education and use that potential wisely. Second, we should recognize that much of the surprising transformation brought about by eighteenth-century hymns occurred almost as an accidental byproduct of the hymnographers' efforts, rather than the primary aim of their work. In this regard, humility and reliance on the Spirit remain indispensable elements in guiding the worship of the church. In the sections that follow, we'll look at these two points in greater detail to see how churches can best approach the use of congregational song as a means of teaching theology and transforming church cultures.

The Power of Congregational Song

What was it that made the songs of Watts and Doddridge such powerful tools for communicating a new missional sensibility? Would the same effects have been attainable by some other means of communication in the eighteenth century, such as a book or a preaching campaign? As we consider the best way to apply these insights to our own day, we might wonder if another mode of offering the same insights—perhaps a video course or podcast—might be just as effective.

While each mode of communication offers potential advantages, songs possess an inherent power that makes them especially useful for conveying a large-scale theological vision, like the idea of global mission. A hymn can't go into the same level of depth or detail as a sermon or a book, but it has built-in advantages for communicating a single big idea or a theological sensibility, while other forms of communication have their own limitations. A sermon series can certainly be useful, but unless all the pastors in a country start preaching the same sermons, the theological vision communicated there is likely to be isolated to a particular church. A book can be published widely, but its influence is still likely to be muted in comparison to a set of hymns because most books only reach a select audience, are read once, and then put away, while a song can gain repeated exposure with a wide audience. If we could point to a rise in missiological thinking attached to an early-eighteenth-century book, that would be notable, but one would still not expect the influence of its ideas to have spread as quickly or as broadly as did the ideas woven into the popular hymns of the day.

Hymnody's power to teach, persuade, and shape congregational thought was already recognized at the very beginning of the Golden Age of Hymns. The hymnographers of the eighteenth century understood their hymns to be instruments of both pedagogy and praise, crafting their songs with theological instruction in mind.[1] Hymns could serve as mini-sermons in poetic form, communicating

1 Sherman, "Catechetical Function," 84; Johnson, "Is This the Lord's Song?" 195–96.

biblical and theological content, and in their emotionally expressive range, they could even surpass a sermon's engagement with the laity. We know, in fact, that this is where many early Nonconformist hymns originated: pastors seeking a way to reinforce the theological content of their sermons by putting those messages into a sung, repeatable form. A new hymn composed to accompany a sermon would be introduced at the Sunday worship service where that sermon was preached, and then the hymn would be repeated in the worship of the church several times over the ensuing months and years. In this way, the theological content of the hymn was highlighted, placed in its proper biblical context, and reinforced by repetition.[2]

Hymns also have disadvantages when compared with other text-based sources, of course—their structure does not allow for as thorough or as well-articulated a statement of missiological content as a book would—but for the communication of basic ideas and broad theological visions, their form and usage are unmatched. A book introducing the same material would likely struggle to gain widespread readership unless the groundwork had already been laid by the public's familiarity with its perspectives through other, more accessible theological media. This was exactly the process that allowed William Carey's missiological treatise to have such a widespread impact at the time of its publication. The groundwork had already been laid, first by hymns, then by the fervor for evangelism arising from the Evangelical Revival, and finally by the popularization of missions in local pastors' meetings and sermons.

That pattern is not only discernible in the eighteenth century; it has a long lineage in church history. The usefulness of hymns as effective communicators of theological ideas is evident from the apostolic age to our own day. Hymns have been actively employed as theological megaphones many times, including by the fourth-century heresiarch Arius, who sought popular support for his theological positions, as

2 See Payne, "Eighteenth Century English Congregationalism," 199, 292; Deacon, *Philip Doddridge*, 77–78; cf. Lamport, et al., *Hymns and Hymnody*, 199–200, 204.

well as by the great church father Ambrose, who pushed back against the encroachment of Arian doctrines. The Latin Ambrosian hymns of the West went on to have a major influence on Catholic hymnody for the next thousand years, especially as reinforced by Gregorian worship reforms. In the East, the development and popularity of a song form known as *kontakia* in Orthodox churches helped add strength and stability to the devotion of ordinary Christians as they faced the challenges of christological controversies and Islam's first advance in the mid-first millennium AD.[3]

Later, songs as tools of theological pedagogy formed part of the standard practice of the earliest global mission movements. Some Catholic missionaries in the Age of Exploration developed songs to support the catechesis of innumerable new converts in Latin America, India, and elsewhere. The Jesuit missionary Francis Xavier used simple songs and repetitive recitations to teach basic doctrine to the indigenous inhabitants of the places he traveled.[4] It wasn't just Catholics who used hymns as theological teaching-tools; several hymnologists have noted that Protestant groups in particular have made widespread use of hymns as practical vehicles for communicating basic theological principles to the laity—a tradition that dates back to Martin Luther and the roots of the Reformation.[5]

Within the eighteenth century, the hymns of Charles Wesley were an indispensable part of fanning the flames of the Evangelical Revival. In the nineteenth century, a further growth of both revival hymns and mission hymns continued to stoke enthusiasm for the ever-expanding Protestant mission movement and helped produce the Second Great Awakening at the same time. Even in recent decades, the close association of new movements in worship with new areas of growth in the global church is hard to ignore.

---

3 D'Ambrosio, *When the Church Was Young*, 155; Meyendorff, *Imperial Unity*, 76, 99.

4 Melbournensis, "St. Francis Xavier," 343; see also Neill, *History of Christian Missions*, 150.

5 Wootton, "Wilderness and Christian Song," 77; Johnson, "Is This the Lord's Song?" 196.

What makes congregational song such a powerful tool for shaping theological awareness and launching new movements? It has structural advantages over almost any other means of disseminating theological sensibilities. Three main sets of advantages stand out: (1) the public, communal nature of hymns' use; (2) the frequency and repetition of their use; and (3) the memorability inherent in their structural form.

The first aspect of hymnody's usefulness in communicating theological perspectives lies in the communal nature of hymns' usage. It is important to remember that hymns' were not solely tied to the church; they were widely used in homes as well. Family worship times and personal devotions made widespread use of hymns, a practice that stretched from the early eighteenth century to the mid-twentieth. If a family had the means, they would purchase a copy of the hymnbook introduced in their church's services and use those hymns in their own private worship. In this way, the hymns were not limited to the selectivity practiced by a pastor or worship leader; the entire corpus of hymns in a hymnbook could begin to have an effect. And because hymns were employed in both public worship and home settings, they regularly reached very broad audiences.[6] This broad-based reach of hymnody, finding its first major dissemination in public and then reinforced in private use, contrasts with a book, which must depend either on the slow process of reaching one reader at a time or on the rare happenstance of having its material taken up and popularized in sermons or lectures.

In addition to promoting a numerically broad reach, the communal aspect of hymns' usage has another effect. Since it is, by nature, something that Christians do together, and since its form is so highly geared toward this unitive action, congregational singing communicates a sense of its own importance to Christian identity. Christians are people who sing together, and since singing together adds an element of harmony to the life of the body of Christ, those songs come to be honored as something especially precious in the lives

6 See Terry, Smith, and Anderson, *Missiology*, 560–61; Phillips, *Hymnal*, 205.

of many Christians. With this place of honor given to congregational songs, such that they become beloved expressions of what it means to be a part of the church, the meanings interwoven in their texts will come to have an outsized effect on the theological sensibilities of the individual Christians who use them.

By using a medium grounded in the public worship of the church, hymns become a part of the liturgy. The early church recognized that it was the liturgy, the worship of the gathered church, that shaped, upheld, and reinforced the doctrines of the church community. Their saying was, "*Lex orandi, lex credendi*"—"the rule of prayer is the rule of faith." That is to say, the regular worship of the church—which includes its songs, prayers, and especially the faithful reading and teaching of Scripture—molds the shape and expression of the church's faith. By enshrining hymn texts in the public life of the church, the theological messages within them become part of the church's self-understanding.[7] This means, on one hand, that the theology of songs and hymns should not be approached lightly, without serious reflection on the doctrines and sensibilities conveyed in the songs, and on the other hand, it offers a tremendously powerful tool for building awareness of certain crucial doctrines in the life of the church.

The second aspect undergirding hymnody's utility as a theological medium is its frequency of usage. Most of the early hymnographers, including Watts and Doddridge, were pastors who expressly designed their hymns to be both theologically educational and suitable for repeated use.[8] As these texts are sung repeatedly, the messages they contain become familiar. Hymns thus have a unique ability to shape the theological mentality of a congregation over many years, even generations. Repeated exposure to the same perspective makes it more likely for that perspective to sink into the minds of those who

7 See Wootton, "Wilderness and Christian Song," 77; Johnson, "Is This the Lord's Song?" 196; Eskew and McElrath, *Sing with Understanding*, 59.

8 See Johnson, "Is This the Lord's Song?" 195–96; Payne, "Eighteenth Century English Congregationalism," 292.

use it, and thus more likely that a missiological theme from a popular hymn would gradually become an ever-more conscious part of the theological worldview of the Nonconformist community.

The *Psalms of David Imitated,* in particular, managed to harness the advantage of frequent repetition in congregational and family worship because they were based on the already established practice of using psalms as congregational songs. Many people who would have otherwise been hesitant to swap out psalms for hymns found a compromise in using Watts's psalm-imitations, which led to the skyrocketing popularity of his hymns.[9] The self-reinforcing and self-perpetuating aspects of hymnody ensured that new missiological expressions arising from the underlying psalms would be repeated and reused until they became part of the broader Nonconformist perspective on the world.

Furthermore, Isaac Watts, Joseph Stennett, and other hymnographers composed hymns for particular rites of the church, like communion and baptism, thus increasing the likelihood of repeated use.[10] In fact, several hymns composed for baptism are among the most missiologically rich, because they quote the Great Commission from the end of Matthew, thanks to its reference to baptism. Thus it came about that whenever Nonconformists held a baptism, they sang hymns directly linked to Jesus's command for worldwide mission.

Even in a demonination that was not itself very missionally oriented, the frequent repetition of such a text would, over time, have a significant effect on the laity's understanding of the Christian life. Rather than being a neglected biblical text (which it was for much of church history), the Great Commission began to stand out in people's minds as an important part of Scripture, central to the church's work in

9 Herzel, *To Thee We Sing*, 142; Gillman, *Evolution of the English Hymn*, 211; Davie, *Gathered Church*, 33–34.

10 See Lamport, et al., *Hymns and Hymnody*, 165; Wykes, "From David's Psalms," 234; Watts, *Dissenters*, 310.

the world.[11] It was, in fact, during this very time period—the eighteenth century—that the use of the Great Commission as a motivating text for global mission truly burst into the Christian consciousness. It is perhaps more than a coincidence, then, that the Great Commission suddenly became recognized as the church's central missiological text in those very church communions that had started singing it together every time they had a baptism.

The third aspect of hymnody's usefulness in communicating theological ideas is its memorability. By using the tools of rhyme, meter, and melody, hymn texts amplify their impact significantly. Putting a text in poetic and musical form makes it relatively easy to memorize.[12] Unlike a spoken text, which must be repeated and consciously memorized, a musical text is remembered fairly rapidly and with relatively little effort, especially if used frequently. This is common knowledge, and it works, as any Kindergarten teacher will tell you. Putting your pedagogy in song form helps it stick in the learners' minds. Hymns even tend to have an edge over other rhymed musical texts, like metrical psalms, when it comes to their ability to be easily memorized. Hymns are often shorter than metrical psalms, more thematically unified, and in most cases, use affective language and sensibilities more familiar to the singer's own culture, all of which will tend toward easier memorization.

The memorization of texts has a long association with pedagogical techniques in both Christian and secular historical contexts. In some Nonconformist circles (as with many other Christian groups), the memorization of Bible verses or catechism answers was a widely accepted form of Christian pedagogy, based on the belief that memorization aided in the internalization of a text's meaning and its application to one's life.[13] Similarly, Western educational methods,

11 Wright, "Great Commission," 153–5; Parris, *Reading the Bible*, 122; Boer, *Pentecost and Missions*, 15; Bosch, "Structure of Mission," 218.

12 See Terry, Smith, and Anderson, *Missiology*, 561.

13 Sherman, "Catechetical Function," 80.

from ancient Roman tutors to twentieth-century grammar schools, regularly highlighted the importance of having students commit notable texts to memory.[14] Since hymns are structured to facilitate easy memorization, it follows that they would provide users the same pedagogical benefits associated with the memorization of other texts. If memorization aids with internalizing a text's meaning, then one could assume that the memorability of hymns would enhance their ability to gradually shape users' theological perspectives in line with the hymns' missiological content.

The unique combination of structural factors in hymnody—texts which are intentionally designed for biblical and theological pedagogy, crafted for frequent repetition in congregational use, and set to music—makes hymns an ideal medium for disseminating new ways of thinking about the Christian life. Any missiological content in early Nonconformist hymns would tend to become self-reinforcing, embedding itself ever more into a congregation's understanding of Christian living and shaping its attitude and rhetoric toward issues they might not otherwise have considered, such as the spiritual state of non-Christian populations around the world.

With these aspects of hymnody's utility in mind, it appears very likely that the missiological themes in Watts's and Doddridge's hymns had an expansive impact on the mindset of eighteenth-century Nonconformism. As hymnologists Harry Eskew and Hugh McElrath state, "The basic beliefs of most Christians have been formulated more by the hymns they sing than by the preaching they hear or the Bible study they pursue."[15] If that is the case, then a direct line can be drawn from the missiological themes of early Nonconformist hymns to the foundational ideas of the Protestant mission movement.

14 See Shiner, "On the Memorisation of Poetry," 108–10.

15 Eskew and McElrath, *Sing with Understanding*, 59.

Choosing Songs for Theological Pedagogy

This first element that emerges from the story of eighteenth-century hymnody—the sheer power of congregational song to shape the theological vision of a church body—offers lessons for pastors and liturgists who seek to use it well. Since it can be such an effective tool, worship leaders should make discerning choices in their church's ministry of song.

The first major application is directed toward contemporary composers of congregational songs. The message here is simple: Write songs with diligent intentionality regarding their theological meanings and their potential for encouraging missional engagement. The findings of this research suggest that hymnography can be one of the chief means of developing and maintaining missional cultures in local church networks. Whether through the composition of classic-style hymns or newer models of congregational song, the church will benefit from an expanded recognition of the didactic power of hymnography as a tool for theological immersion. It is worth noting that many missionary agencies now regularly include cross-cultural musicologists as part of their global engagement teams. This practice—intentionally crafting a culture of indigenous song, filled with theological and missional themes appropriate to one's local context—has become a normal part of global Christian outreach. This ought to be the case not only for newly developing areas of Christian expansion but also for church networks that already have long-established traditions of congregational song.

Songs can be effective tools for prompting people to think about global mission, local outreach, or vocational ministry more frequently than they might through the preaching ministry of a church. The reception of a call to ministry, for example, often finds its initial preparatory framework in the life of the local congregation, where music plays an important role. The infusion of a rich vein of missiological thought into the musical liturgy of established Christian traditions can provide a vehicle for vocational preparation within the local church, inspiring young people to consider employing their gifts for the sake of God's kingdom work in their own communities and around the world.

The lessons of eighteenth-century hymnography also encourage us to highlight local participation in composing songs for worship. Much of the songwriting process has become centralized and industrialized over the past few decades, emphasizing those artists and groups with the talent and resources to reach broad audiences. However, there can also be a place for local-church hymnography alongside participation in the wider trends of Christian worship. The hymnographers of early Nonconformism wrote their hymns primarily for use in their own local congregations, and much of their appeal derived from the fact that they were adapted to local cultures of worship. It remained common throughout the eighteenth and nineteenth centuries for local pastors and lay poets to compose their own songs for congregational use alongside those available in published hymnals, and what remains in circulation is just a small portion of the vast treasure trove of hymns written during those centuries.

Such a culture of local hymnography allows ecclesial communities to reflect on the specific theological themes they want to emphasize in their congregational life and to develop musical liturgies for presenting and maintaining those themes. My own church in Maine has records of several original hymns composed by lay poets in our congregation in the mid-1800s, used in worship on special occasions. These songs are a precious record of the way God was working at the time, not only in the world at large but in our own little corner of the kingdom.

Composers of congregational songs, both those whose works reach millions and those serving their own local communities, should consider the power of song in shaping ecclesial culture and pursue their work with theological integrity and intentionality. The work of eighteenth-century hymnographers suggests a method for this endeavor: let Scripture lead the way. Almost all the hymns of the eighteenth century were rooted in the Word of God, either as paraphrases or expositions of a biblical text. In the cases of Watts and Doddridge, as pastors engaged in the weekly teaching ministry of the church, most of their hymns emerged from deep reflection and prayer on the appointed Bible passages for the week. The composition of songs for worship was undertaken less as an exercise in seeking content that would capture broad appeal in the worship music market and more as a prayerful immersion in the biblically rooted life of the local church.

If the first major application of this research is simply an encouragement to write theologically rich songs, the second application focuses on clergy and worship leaders who may not write their own songs but select the songs used in worship. Given the thousands of hymns and worship songs available to churches today, how can one structure an intentional program of theological pedagogy in the weekly worship of a congregation?

To engage with congregational song in a manner that recognizes its capacity for theological immersion, it is advisable for leaders to consider the theological merits of the songs regularly used. Using a method similar to the content analysis in this research, leaders can assess the hymns and songs currently in use according to a theological scale of their own design, ensuring that their selection provides thorough and robust coverage of the themes deemed important for that ecclesial community.

The easiest way to do this requires a basic level of preparation and intentionality: working through the corpus of songs in regular use in one's congregation, noting their main theological emphases, and tracking how often certain themes are presented to the church. By noting the frequency of certain types of songs, one can prepare a cycle of songs that emphasizes whatever one's central theological focus might be: Trinitarian doctrine, Christology, salvation theology, sanctification, missiology, etc.

This approach might seem strangely analytical to some, but it has the benefit of preventing the common slide into lax worship that so many churches experience simply using whatever is most familiar or appealing at a whim. By intentionally thinking through which theological themes to emphasize and regularly cycling through songs that reflect those themes, one mitigates the dangers of a shallow liturgy of song. This kind of intentionality replaces a system that aims for the lowest common denominator and instead enacts a system that will challenge, invigorate, and inspire the church through repeated use.

It should be noted, however, that if one wants to approach the subject even more analytically, it's possible to do so. Not everyone will care to engage with the system outlined below, but for a few enterprising souls who enjoy collecting and analyzing data, it might prove interesting and helpful. The following process is based on the content analysis model that undergirds this book's research, which is detailed in the full dissertation available online.[16] (And if you're not one of the people who would find such a system interesting, please feel free to skip down to the next section header.)

To design a complete theological assessment of congregational song, a leader would need to follow three simple steps. The first step is to select an accessible source document upon which to base one's content analysis. While some leaders might be tempted to select the Bible for this exercise, it would likely result in a content analysis system that is both too complicated and too open to personal interpretation to be useful. A good source document would either focus on a specific field, like missiology, or be marked by its theological accessibility, such as a creed, confession, or mission statement. For this book's research, the source document for the content analysis was William Carey's *Enquiry*, which had the advantage of being relatively brief while still providing comprehensive coverage of the missiological themes at play in the Protestant mission movement.

A church leader desiring to highlight songs with missiological content in contemporary church life might be advised to choose a more contemporary text, of which there are numerous good examples

16 Burden, "Emergence and Development," https://research.sats.ac.za/browse/author.

available. In many cases, however, a church leader will likely seek a set of songs that reflects not just a certain missiological perspective, but a comprehensive immersion in the doctrines of their church's theological tradition. In such a case, it may be best to consider that tradition's creeds, confessions, or doctrinal statements as possible source documents.

The second step, once a source document is selected, is to proceed with the content analysis process. This is done by categorizing each theological theme in the source document as a "code" to be analyzed for its presence in the corpus of songs. A list of theological themes can be as long or as short as necessary, but it tends to be most effective if it does not exceed twenty such "codes."

The third step, once one has a list of theological themes from the source document, involves assessing a corpus of songs for the frequency and comprehensiveness of their usage of those themes. The researcher will work through the text of the songs, noting the appearance of the coded themes as they arise. Each theme's appearance is recorded, resulting in a data set that shows which themes appear across the corpus, how frequently they appear, and which songs have the greatest frequency and distribution of particular themes. The content analysis model allows leaders to consider how frequently certain important doctrines are presented to the congregation through the fruitful, culture-building means of communal song, and to select those songs that will have the greatest effect—not only with regard to emotional impact and personal enjoyment, which are so often the driving motivators for song choice, but also for the purpose of inculcating theological richness into the church's worship.

While it might sound too black-and-white to apply an analytical process to fields like theology and song, this model has certain merits worth considering. A method like this encourages liturgists to build a helpful list of the theological themes they deem important to the life of the church and to remain cognizant of the full scope of those themes in their selections for congregational song. Without the application of such a method, the rotation of songs used in worship can be guided more by the whim of the moment than by a sense of theological intentionality. Even if a certain thematic area appears regularly in a church's songs, it likely will not receive the same kind of comprehensive thematic coverage that can result from a more intentional approach, like the one outlined here. This method, in contrast to the typical approach, promotes thoughtful preparation in worship in a way that allows the songs of the church to serve as culture-building tools for the entire set of theological themes valued in that church's communion, and not merely a subset of them.

Walking in Step with the Spirit

In the previous section, we laid out two sets of practical applications for pastors and worship leaders: to be active in writing songs and to practice intentionality in choosing songs for public worship. In this section, we must consider another lesson that comes to us from the story of eighteenth-century hymnography: how to reckon with the accidental (or better, the providential) nature of its effects—something that cannot be induced by any level of preparation or intentionality.

This is especially true when we consider the titanic impact of Isaac Watts's *Psalms of David Imitated* on the missiological thinking of Nonconformist churches. As shown in the preceding chapters, Watts's hymn texts, which were missiologically rich, were the result of combining biblical content with a particular hymn-writing method, rather than from his own missional awareness. Those themes emerged, as it were, by accident, and yet those accidents provided the most fruitful fields for the Spirit's work during the Golden Age of Hymns. So when we think about how to apply such lessons to our own practice, it may seem like we are faced with an impossible question: How can we stumble into happy accidents that engage the Spirit's work in ways we cannot yet foresee?

There are two practical answers to this question: a Bible-centered answer and an ecclesiological answer. The first answer notes that most of Watts's and Doddridge's unintended positive effects were achieved by plumbing the Scriptures for the content of their hymns. The development of missiological content in early hymns appears to have been largely unintentional, the result of Watts's appropriation and application of biblical themes from the psalms, a work that was then carried forward (with a bit more foresight and intentionality) by Doddridge. This unique fusion of biblical content with the didactic power of hymnography laid the groundwork for a movement of such scope that it altered the course of global Christianity.

Among the leading concerns, then, for composers of congregational song, should be the incorporation of biblical content. If we believe in the efficacy of Scripture—that every word is God-breathed and does not return to him void—then it seems an obvious conclusion that Scripture will provide us with the greatest fruitfulness for rich theological songs. Aside from the clear fact that God commits to speak through his Word, basing the content of our songs on Scripture may result in the reappropriation of theological themes that, due to our cultural blind spots, we may not even be aware of yet. Just like eighteenth-century English Christianity tended to have a blind spot regarding the call of global mission—a blind spot exposed by the missiological content of the psalms communicated through hymns—there may be similar blind spots that we hold, which Scripture can illuminate for us.

It should be noted, though, that it wasn't just a case of taking Bible verses and setting them to music, as useful as that can be. Most of the transformative impact of eighteenth-century hymns emerged from the process of biblical texts being considered, prayed over, and applied to the practice of the Christian life. The preceding two centuries of singing metrical psalms, despite their richness and beauty, had not produced a similar effect. Watts, Doddridge, and other hymnographers approached their craft as sermons in song, reflecting a resolution not just to hear the Word of God, but to explain it and apply it as best as they could. Thus, Bible songs (like metrical psalms) are akin to the public reading of Scripture—a necessary and fruitful part of any Christian service—but hymns are more akin to sermons, in which the text is used to move, inspire, and instruct the congregation as it is applied to their lives.

Composers of congregational songs could consider an ancient Christian practice of devotional creativity as a way to approach their songwriting: the Orthodox art of iconography. To the Eastern Orthodox, painting (or, as it is often phrased, "writing") a religious icon is more an exercise of prayer than creativity. It is an art form suffused with prayer from beginning to end, which aims for the actual communication of the divine grace present in the story of the gospel. It grounds itself in inclining the heart toward God as part of the writing process, not merely in the public display and usage the piece receives. It also seeks to faithfully transmit the reality of what is portrayed, and thus Bible characters, saints, and biblical stories are represented in ways that are faithful both to Scripture and to the wisdom of tradition.[17] To write hymns or songs in this way, then, is to make prayer and Scripture the pillars of the process, seeking to faithfully employ the words and ideas of Scripture in the song and invoking the Lord's blessing on every step of the process.

Beyond the practice of using Scripture, a second answer arises to the question of how we might position ourselves to receive happy accidents in our use of hymns. This answer—an ecclesiological one—is the same principle often repeated in the letters of Revelation: to hear what the Spirit is saying to the churches. One of the interesting features of worship in the eighteenth century was that it involved the introduction of a new form of congregational song, a form that was controversial at first. Some churches and communions tended not to embrace the new hymns, deriding them as merely "men's composures."[18] It is worth noting that those ecclesiastical communions which chose to ignore this new form of worship were also the communions that

17 Martin, *Sacred Doorways*, xv–5, 215–16.

18 See Davies, *Worship and Theology*, 126–27.

missed out on the rich missiological ferment of the hymn texts, and thus later found themselves a generation or two behind when it came to the great Protestant mission movement. By contrast, those churches that did pay attention to the arrival of this new form of congregational song, those that weighed its dangers and merits and opted for a discerning use of the new form, were the same churches that ended up standing at the forefront of the missionary advance.

That's not to say that we should be running after every new trend that becomes popular in some random wing of the global church. But it should remind us that we are called to be people who have our eyes and ears open, watchful and listening for the Spirit, so that when new movements in worship do arise, we can engage them with discernment, wisdom, and courage. Within the lived experience of Christians today, we have seen major movements toward both the unhindered, emotive forms of Pentecostal worship, which has been a significant factor in the explosive growth of Christianity in some parts of the world, as well as a tidal shift among young Christians in the West who are seeking the timeless, ancient rhythms of liturgical worship. The wisdom of history would advise us not to dismiss either movement too quickly, but to recognize the fruits of the Spirit's work in them and to engage with their strengths while also guarding against their weaknesses.

This is a matter for careful discernment. Not every new movement in worship produces positive effects in the church. Sometimes innovations in worship have been promoted for purely sectarian purposes, aiming to use the power of music to advocate for a divisive doctrinal stance. For example, this happened at the turn of the sixth century, when Non-Chalcedonians tried to sway theological debates by introducing a modified version of the classic Trisagion song (adding the following line in italics: "Holy God, Holy Mighty, Holy Immortal One / Who was crucified for us / Have mercy on us").[19] Even the influence of Watts and Doddridge came under significant criticism.

---

19 Meyendorff, *Imperial Unity*, 200.

While their hymns were not intended to erase the church's tradition of psalmody, they ended up having that effect. Almost all English Protestants gradually switched from singing psalms to singing hymns (though there were a few exceptions), resulting in a decline in the church's familiarity with the biblical psalms.[20] Even as we appreciate the monumental achievement in Watts's and Doddridge's hymns, it might be worth considering whether we could, at the same time, retrieve some of the wealth that has been lost in the abandonment of psalmody.

Since we are thinking about the dangers associated with new forms of worship, we ought to address one of the most troubling critiques of early English hymnody—one that some people point to as clear evidence of negative effects arising from this worship movement. Later generations would look back and criticize the mission hymns of the period for the part they played in the imperialist legacy of European expansion.[21] It is true that European colonialism was a morally dubious venture that had many negative effects on the nations affected by it, and furthermore, that some of the mission hymns of the Christian church would come to be perceived as triumphal pieces of imperialist propaganda.

This particular criticism, though, is mostly an anachronism when directed against the earliest hymnographers, like Watts and Doddridge. The criticism assumes that the colonialist mentality of the mid-nineteenth century was common in the early decades of the eighteenth, but this was generally untrue in the case of the Nonconformists, who had few connections to the political and commercial enterprises that drove Britain's ever-expanding reach.[22] In fact, the Nonconformist churches of the eighteenth century were quite distant from the racist or patronizing motivations occasionally attributed to them. When they considered the global spread of Christianity at all (which, as we have seen, was not often), they were

20 Herzel, *To Thee We Sing*, 142; Gillman, *Evolution of the English Hymn*, 211.

21 See Lamport, et al., *Hymns and Hymnody*, 287.

22 See Bosch, *Transforming Mission*, 310; Neill, *History of Christian Missions*, 261.

driven less by the nineteenth-century idea of promoting "civilization" and more by the implicit missiology of Scripture.

We have records of some Nonconformist-aligned Christians of the period, like Jonathan Edwards (who, remember, had close ties to Watts and Doddridge), urging a consideration of global mission not just for the spiritual good of those who have never heard the gospel, but for the health and strength of the English and American churches. Edwards had the foresight to argue that people from other cultures would necessarily bring edifying new perspectives into the global church. In this view, the missionary-sending nation was as much a recipient of the blessings of mission as the receiving nation was, to the extent that England and America stood in need of the strengths that unreached peoples would bring to the faith. In his *History of Redemption,* Edwards put it like this:

> It may be hoped, then, that many of the Negroes and Indians will be divines [that is, great teachers of Christian doctrine], and that excellent books will be published in Africa, in Ethiopia, in Tartary, and other now the most barbarous countries; and not only learned men, but others of more ordinary education, shall then be very knowing in religion. There shall then be a wonderful unravelling of the difficulties in the doctrines of religion, and clearing up of seeming inconsistencies: "Lo, crooked things shall be made strait, and rough places shall be made plain, and darkness shall become light before God's people." Difficulties in Scripture shall then be cleared up, and wonderful things shall be discovered in the word of God, which were never discovered before.[23]

We must thus conduct mission not only for the sake of "the other" but for our own sakes, because among those many "others" are future teachers, leaders, and doctors of the church, whose wisdom and

23 Edwards, *Works of President Edwards,* Vol. 3, 405–6.

insights we ourselves will need. This is not an imperialist mentality but a kingdom mentality. It was only much later that external social developments led people to start hearing and reading the early hymns, like "Jesus Shall Reign," in a specifically colonial sense.

Even if the colonial critique is largely misplaced when leveled against early Nonconformist hymnody, other examples of negative influences from movements in Christian worship are not hard to find. It has been a decades-long critique of the now-ubiquitous praise-and-worship style that it has traded robust theological content for sheer emotionalism. While that critique is often overblown, most people can think of popular and influential worship songs that fit that description. A common poster child for this criticism is the overly repetitive "I Could Sing of Your Love Forever," popular near the turn of the twenty-first century. The truth is, though, that similar trends favoring emotiveness over theological content are easy to find even in the hymns of the preceding generations, as seen in the steadfastly popular hymn "In the Garden."

There is a legitimate fear that such songs can contribute to an embrace of the modern American heresy, which centers one's faith not on the all-majestic holiness of the God of the Bible but on the idea of a God who exists to seek the worshiper's individual fulfillment. This produces an overstated focus on one's own emotions in the Christian life, which follows the general belief that God wants you to be happy. This is an obviously shallow, oversimplified view of Christianity, and it is justly approached with caution.

These issues remind us of the importance of practicing careful discernment amid our engagement with new worship movements. But that doesn't necessarily mean that shunning such movements is required. History warns us about how we approach such issues. Many liturgists throughout the ages—including the eighteenth century—have spent their lives bemoaning the weaknesses of new forms of worship, and in retrospect, their endeavors look like a case of willful blindness to the evident strengths of those same forms. Church history is full of sad stories of those who make their reaction against a form of worship the main element of their own practice and end up with a negative, narrow, legalistic version of Christian life. Examples of this range from the iconoclasts of the early medieval church to the social media polemicists of today, who make their living by compiling lists of worship artists whose songs must be avoided at all costs.

While there is certainly a danger inherent in songs that emphasize emotionalism over theological depth, that danger only truly materializes if such songs are used to the exclusion of all others. The answer is probably not to get rid of such songs altogether but to seek a balance with other styles, forms, or songs. There is a place for the beauty of emotive expressions in Christian worship, especially if the strengths of theologically rich songs can compensate for the weaknesses of other songs. A church that can use both "I Could Sing of Your Love Forever" and "Love Divine, All Loves Excelling" is perhaps in a better position than churches that opt for merely one or the other, because the former churches retain the strengths of both kinds of songs, which speak in different ways to different hearts (and such churches require congregants who are wired differently to learn how to love each other, too, which is no small thing).

Indeed, Isaac Watts himself, a proponent of logical thinking and deep theology, also argued forcefully for the legitimate place of affective expression in the worship of the church.[24] What is called for here is not a black-and-white categorization of songs and styles into good or bad, but a recognition of the strengths and weaknesses of each form and a willingness to practice balanced discernment in the worship of the church. Multiple styles and forms of sung worship exist in the church because each form has proven useful in expressing the praise of the people of God, and trying to eliminate one of those forms will likely prove just as ineffective as those who, in the eighteenth century, wanted to abolish the use of the new hymnody.

---

24 Gant, *History of English Church Music*, 240–41; Rogal, *General Introduction*, 86; Beynon, "Helpfulness of the Lesser Known Work," 482.

So, to return to the main point of this section: If we are looking for models to emulate from the worship of eighteenth-century England, it would seem that the best model of engaging with new forms of worship comes from those Nonconformist churches that recognized the strengths of the new hymns and embraced them. Some of those churches also retained, at the same time, a robust usage of metrical psalms, so it certainly wasn't an all-or-nothing choice for one form or the other.

It would behoove us, then, to consider the worship movements in our own day, from the continued prominence of emotionally evocative praise songs to the revival of richly theological hymn-style songs, to the broad wave of people turning from evangelical worship to more classically liturgical forms. In each instance, it would be well to hear what the Spirit is saying to the churches, to consider each form discerningly and engage with its strengths while remaining mindful of possible dangers. This clear-eyed openness is nothing new or revolutionary; it is simply the posture of those who seek to be both faithful to the truth handed down to them and actively engaged in the ongoing movement of God's work in the world.

The history of eighteenth-century Nonconformism shows the potential connections between congregational song and major movements of missional outreach. By reappropriating the biblical text and applying it to contemporary Christian life in the medium of song, Isaac Watts and Philip Doddridge were able to prepare the ground in their circle of churches for the blossoming of a major mission movement, one that changed the course of history. Should today's church leaders, hymnwriters, and liturgists follow their model, the songs of the people of God might again prove to be the catalysts for major movements yet to come.

Conclusion

The story of the Protestant mission movement is one that has long been known to students of mission. Many of the root inspirations for the launch of global Protestant missions are already well understood and analyzed in numerous books by scholars in the field. Those studies elucidated the important contributions of early missionaries among the Lutherans, Moravians, and American colonists, as well as the fresh wave of evangelical zeal that emerged in the mid-eighteenth-century revivals. However, the picture thus portrayed has not been complete; there remain some missing pieces to the puzzle.

One of those missing pieces—and, I would argue, a crucial one—is the role played by the revolution in worship that emerged in Baptist and Congregationalist churches in the decades before the mission movement. The hymns of Isaac Watts and Philip Doddridge had begun instilling a new missional vision into the hearts and minds of churchgoers for more than half a century before that vision took shape. The almost unwitting nature of that contribution—unintended but massively effective—suggests that it represents one of the many hidden threads of God's providential work in the history of his church.

This is the story not only of a small group of churches and their global impact but also of the Holy Spirit's work in history. The historian typically avoids any claim of pinpointing the Spirit's activity, since doing so usually means stretching one's evidence too far. Some historians—particularly those interested in demonstrating divine favor toward their own denominational story—have fallen into the trap of cherry-picking historical evidence to fit their own beliefs, rather than allowing the story of the church to stand on its own. Here, as in many cases, it is too easy to stumble into the fallacy of confirmation bias, where one finds evidence for the position one was looking for and then stamps the imprint of the Spirit's activity onto it as a divine endorsement.

The Spirit's activity is not always easy to discern, especially from an impartial viewpoint. As Jesus told Nicodemus, it is rather like the wind—one can observe its effects, but the wind itself moves by a mystery hidden from human eyes. On the other hand, the Spirit is always and everywhere at work in the body of Christ, and, just like the wind, it is hard to look at the grand sweep of movements and missions across the world and not see the effects of Pentecost's wind still blowing through the church. So every now and then, when one looks at church history, one can catch just a flash, a sideways glimmer, of the Spirit on the move.

The story told in these pages offers one such glimpse of the Holy Spirit at work in the history of the church. From a wave of new worship arose a wave of new mission, and most startlingly, that mission appeared to find its inspiration from the words of a man who scarcely thought of mission at all—the great hymnographer Isaac Watts. Yet by a kind of blind serendipity, he wrote a collection of hymns that brought the call of global mission back to the forefront of the Christian mind, and so—unforeseen and unplanned—worship led to mission.

If one is looking for signs of the Spirit's work, this odd coincidence appears more like providence than chance. It is, in fact, just the sort of pattern we should expect to find. From the book of Acts onward, mission emerges as the fruit of the communal worship of the church. The Jerusalem church worshiped and prayed together, and thousands were added to their number. The church of Antioch fasted and prayed, and Paul and Barnabas were appointed for missionary service. The early monks set out to establish new centers for the worship of Christ on the fringes of civilization, and in so doing, they became the vanguard of medieval missions. Envoys of a medieval Russian king observed the worship of the churches in Constantinople and were so moved by the experience that they convinced their king and nation to convert to the Christian faith.

Throughout the history of the church, worship and mission are repeatedly linked. Where the church gathers for worship, there the Holy Spirit mobilizes hearts and minds for God's will to be done in the world, and the seeds for new missions are planted. It should come as no surprise, then, that one of the greatest waves of missionary activity the world has ever seen—the Protestant mission movement launched in the late eighteenth century—finds its roots in the worship of the church. Like the river that flowed from the temple's altar in Ezekiel's vision, encompassing the world (Ezek 47), mission flows outward from the worship of the people of God.

The songs we sing together instruct the mind and inspire the heart, preparing us for the great works God has in store for us. Worship and mission have gone hand in hand throughout the history of the church. And ultimately, our great mission of making Christ known to the ends of the earth will find its full-circle fulfillment in worship, when people of every tribe and tongue and nation will surround the throne and, with one voice, cry out together: "Worthy is the Lamb!"

Bibliography

Akin, Daniel L., Benjamin L. Merkle, and George G. Robinson. *40 Questions About the Great Commission*. Kregel Academic, 2020.

Armstrong, Anthony. *The Church of England, the Methodists, and Society*. Rowman & Littlefield, 1973.

Bailey, Albert Edward. *The Gospel in Hymns: Backgrounds and Interpretations*. Charles Scribner's Sons, 1950.

Baxter, Richard. *The Reformed Pastor.* 1656. Repr. Banner of Truth, 1976.

Bebbington, D. W. *Evangelicalism in Modern Britain: A History from the 1730s to the 1980s*. Routledge, 2002.

Beeching, Jack. *An Open Path: Christian Missionaries, 1515–1914*. Ross-Erikson Publishers, 1982.

Bennett, Arthur. *The Valley of Vision: A Collection of Puritan Prayers and Devotions*. Banner of Truth, 1975.

Benson, Louis F. "The Early Editions of Watts's Hymns." *Journal of the Presbyterian Historical Society* 1 (1902): 265–79.

Benson, Louis F. *The English Hymn: Its Development and Use in Worship*. 1915. Repr. John Knox, 1962.

Beveridge, William. *A Defence of the Book of Psalms, Collected into English Metre, by Thomas Sternhold, John Hopkins, and Others*. London, 1710.

Beynon, Graham. "The Helpfulness of the Lesser Known Work: Isaac Watts on the Passions." *Themelios* 42 (2017): 479–93.

Beynon, Graham. *Isaac Watts: His Life and Thought*. Christian Focus Publications, 2013.

Beynon, Graham. *Isaac Watts: Reason, Passion, and the Revival of Religion*. T&T Clark, 2016.

Bickham, Troy O. *Savages Within the Empire: Representations of American Indians in Eighteenth-Century Britain*. Clarendon, 2005.

Binns, John. "Introduction." In *Cyril of Scythopolis: The Lives of the Monks of Palestine*, iv–lii. Cistercian Publications, 1991.

Bishop, Selma L. *Isaac Watts, Hymns and Spiritual Songs, 1707–1748: A Study in Early Eighteenth Century Language Changes*. The Faith Press, 1962.

Blanning, Tim. *The Pursuit of Glory: Europe, 1648–1815*. Viking, 2007.

Boer, Harry R. *Pentecost and Missions*. Eerdmans, 1961.

Bond, Douglas. *The Poetic Wonder of Isaac Watts*. Reformation Trust, 2013.

Bosch, David J. "The Structure of Mission: An Exposition of Matthew 28:16–20." In *Exploring Church Growth*, edited by Wilbert R. Shenk, 218–48. Eerdmans, 1983.

Bosch, David J. *Transforming Mission: Paradigm Shifts in Theology of Mission*. Twentieth anniversary edition. Orbis Books, 2011.

Bosch, David J. *Witness to the World: The Christian Mission in Theological Perspective*. Marshall, Morgan & Scott, 1980.

Brawley, Benjamin. "English Hymnody and Romanticism." *Sewanee Review* 24 (1916): 476–85.

Bray, Gerald. *Anglicanism: A Reformed Catholic Tradition*. Lexham Press, 2021.

Bready, J. Wesley. *England Before and After Wesley: The Evangelical Revival and Social Reform*. 1939. Repr. Regent College Publishing, 2021.

Brockett, Allan. *Nonconformity in Exeter, 1650–1875*. Manchester University Press, 1962.

Browne, Simon. *Hymns and Spiritual Songs*. London, 1720.

Bulman, William J. *Anglican Enlightenment: Orientalism, Religion and Politics in England and Its Empire, 1648–1715*. Cambridge University Press, 2015.

Bunkowske, Eugene W. "Missiology, What Is It?" *Missio Apostolica* 1 (1993): 67–69.

Burden, Matthew. "The Emergence and Development of Missiological Themes in Early Nonconformist Hymnody, 1706–1755." PhD diss., South African Theological Seminary, 2023. https://research.sats.ac.za/browse/author.

Burden, Matthew. *Missionary Motivations: Challenges from the Early Church*. William Carey Publishing, 2023.

Buschart, W. David. *Exploring Protestant Traditions: An Invitation to Theological Hospitality*. IVP Academic, 2006.

Calamy, Edmund. *An Abridgment of Mr Baxter's History of His Life and Times*. 2nd ed. London, 1713.

Calamy, Edmund. *A Continuation of the Account of the Ministers, Lecturers, Masters and Fellows of Colleges and Schoolmasters, Who Were Ejected and Silenced After the Restoration in 1660*. 2 vols. London, 1727.

Carey, S. Pearce. *William Carey*. 8th ed. The Carey Press, 1934.

Carey, William. *An Enquiry into the Obligations of Christians to Use Means for the Conversion of the Heathens*. Leicester, 1792.

Carter, C. Sydney. "Philip Doddridge." *Churchman* 65 (1951): 28–33.

Castleman, Robbie F. "The Last Word: The Great Commission: Ecclesiology." *Themelios* 32, no. 3 (2007): 68–70.

Chute, Anthony L., Nathan A. Finn, and Michael A. G. Haykin. *The Baptist Story: From English Sect to Global Movement*. B&H Academic, 2015.

Colquhoun, Frank. *A Hymn Companion: Insight into Three Hundred Christian Hymns*. Morehouse–Barlow, 1985.

Cousland, Kenneth L. "The Significance of Isaac Watts in the Development of Hymnody." *Church History* 17 (1948): 287–98.

Crawford, Michael J. "Origins of the Eighteenth-Century Evangelical Revival: England and New England Compared." *Journal of British Studies* 26 (1987): 361–97.

D'Ambrosio, Marcellino. *When the Church Was Young: Voices of the Early Fathers*. Franciscan, 2014.

Davie, Donald. *The Eighteenth-Century Hymn in England*. Cambridge University Press, 1993.

Davie, Donald. *A Gathered Church: The Literature of the English Dissenting Interest, 1700–1930*. Oxford University Press, 1978.

Davie, Donald. "The Language of the Eighteenth-Century Hymn." In *English Hymnology in the Eighteenth Century*, edited by Donald Davie and Robert Stevenson, 3–19. University of California, 1980.

Davie, Donald. "Psalmody as Translation." *Modern Language Review* 85 (1990): 817–28.

Davies, Horton. *Worship and Theology in England, Book 2: From Watts and Wesley to Martineau, 1690–1900*. Eerdmans, 1996.

Davis, Arthur Paul. *Isaac Watts: His Life and Works*. London: Independent, 1948.

Deacon, Malcolm. *Philip Doddridge of Northampton, 1702–51*. Northamptonshire Libraries, 1980.

Doddridge, Philip. *An Abridgment of Mr. David Brainerd's Journal Among the Indians*. London, 1748.

Doddridge, Philip. *Free Thoughts on the Most Probable Means of Reviving the Dissenting Interest*. In *The Works of the Reverend P. Doddridge in Ten Volumes*, 199–224. Vol. 4. Leeds, UK, 1803.

Doddridge, Philip. *Hymns Founded on Various Texts in the Holy Scriptures*. Job Orton, ed. Salop, UK, 1755.

Doddridge, Philip. *The Rise and Progress of Religion in the Soul*. 1745. Repr. Religious Tract Society, 1827.

Doddridge, Philip. *Sermons to Young Persons*. London, 1735.

Drewery, Mary. *William Carey: Shoemaker and Missionary*. Hodder & Stoughton, 1978.

Durden, Susan. "Transatlantic Communications and Influence During the Great Awakening: A Comparative Study of British and American Revivalism, 1730–1760." PhD diss., Hull University, 1978.

Edwards, Jonathan. *A Faithful Narrative of the Surprizing Work of God in the Conversion of Many Hundred Souls*. London, 1737.

Edwards, Jonathan. *Religious Affections: A Christian's Character Before God*. Abridgment of *A Treatise Concerning Religious Affections*, 1746. James M. Houston, ed. Regent College Publishing, 2003.

Edwards, Jonathan. *The Works of President Edwards*. Sereno Edwards Dwight, ed. S. Converse, 1829.

Escott, Harry. *Isaac Watts, Hymnographer: A Study of the Beginnings, Development and Philosophy of the English Hymn*. London: Independent, 1962.

Eskew, Harry, and Hugh T. McElrath. *Sing with Understanding: An Introduction to Christian Hymnology*. Broadman Press, 1980.

Etherington, Norman. *Missions and Empire*. Oxford University Press, 2005.

Field, Clive D. "Counting Religion in England and Wales: The Long Eighteenth Century, c.1680–c.1840." *Journal of Ecclesiastical History* 63 (2012): 693–720.

Foote, Henry Wilder. *Three Centuries of American Hymnody*. 1940. Repr. Archon, 1968.

Fountain, David. *Isaac Watts Remembered*. Gospel Standard Trust, 1974.

Freeman, Curtis W. *Undomesticated Dissent: Democracy and the Public Virtue of Religious Nonconformity*. Baylor University Press, 2017.

Gant, Andrew. *A History of English Church Music*. University of Chicago Press, 2017.

George, Timothy. *Faithful Witness: The Life and Mission of William Carey*. New Hope, 1991.

Gibbons, Thomas. *Memoirs of the Rev. Isaac Watts*. London, 1780.

Gillman, Frederick J. *The Evolution of the English Hymn: An Historical Survey of the Origins and Development of the Hymns of the Christian Church*. Macmillan, 1927.

Goheen, Michael W. *Reading the Bible Missionally*. Eerdmans, 2016.

Goodall, Norman. *A History of the London Missionary Society, 1895–1945*. Oxford University Press, 1954.

Goodman, Glenda. "'The Tears I Shed at the Songs of Thy Church': Seventeenth-Century Musical Piety in the English Atlantic World." *Journal of the American Musicological Society* 65 (2012): 691–725.

Grant, William, et al. *Translations and Paraphrases of Several Passages of Sacred Scripture*. Edinburgh, 1745.

Gray, John. *On Hymn Writing*. The English Dominican Order, 1977.

Gray, Scotty. *Hermeneutics of Hymnody: A Comprehensive and Integrated Approach to Understanding Hymns*. Smith & Helwys, 2015.

Greaves, Richard L. "The Puritan-Nonconformist Tradition in England, 1560–1700: Historiographical Reflections." *Albion* 17 (1985): 449–86.

Green, Michael. *Evangelism in the Early Church*. Eerdmans, 1970.

Greene, Jack P. *Evaluating Empire and Confronting Colonialism in Eighteenth-Century Britain*. Cambridge University Press, 2013.

Halley, Robert. *Lancashire: Its Puritanism and Nonconformity*. 2 vols. Manchester, UK, 1869.

Harlan, Lowell B. "Theology of Eighteenth Century English Hymns." *Historical Magazine of the Protestant Episcopal Church* 48 (1979): 167–93.

Harris, F. W. "Philip Doddridge: Eighteenth-Century Ecumenist." *Foundations* 14 (1971): 251–70.

Hart, David Bentley. *The Story of Christianity: A History of 2000 Years of the Christian Faith*. Quercus, 2009.

Heimann, Mary. "Christian Piety in Britain During the 'Long' Nineteenth Century, c.1780–1920." In *Piety and Modernity: The Dynamics of Religious Reform in Northern Europe, 1780–1920*, edited by Anders Jarlert, 27–54. Leuven University Press, 2012.

Herzel, Catherine. *To Thee We Sing*. Muhlenberg, 1946.

Hill, Christopher. *God's Englishman: Oliver Cromwell and the English Revolution*. Harper & Row, 1970.

Hindmarsh, D. Bruce. *The Spirit of Early Evangelicalism: True Religion in a Modern World*. Oxford University Press, 2018.

Hinson, E. Glenn. *The Evangelization of the Roman Empire: Identity and Adaptability*. Mercer University Press, 1981.

Hull, John. "Isaac Watts and the Origins of British Imperial Theology." *International Congregational Journal* 4 (2005): 59–79.

Humphreys, A. R. "Literature and Religion in Eighteenth-Century England." *Journal of Ecclesiastical History* 3 (1952): 159–90.

Humphreys, John Doddridge. *Scriptural Hymns by the Rev. Philip Doddridge, D.D.: New and Corrected Edition, Containing Many Hymns Never Before Printed.* Darton & Clark, 1839.

Hutchinson, William R. *Errand to the World: American Protestant Thought and Foreign Missions.* University of Chicago Press, 1987.

Irvin, Dale T., and Scott W. Sunquist. *History of the World Christian Movement, Vol. 2: Modern Christianity from 1454 to 1800.* Orbis, 2012.

Jacob, W. M. *Lay People and Religion in the Early Eighteenth Century.* Cambridge University Press, 1996.

Jennings, D., and Philip Doddridge. *The Works of the Late Reverend and Learned Isaac Watts.* London, 1753.

Johnson, Dale A. "Is This the Lord's Song? Pedagogy and Polemic in Modern English Hymns." *Historical Magazine of the Protestant Episcopal Church* 48 (1979): 195–218.

Johnson, Paul. *A History of Christianity.* Simon & Schuster, 1976.

Johnson, Samuel. *The Lives of the English Poets.* London, 1820.

Kaul, Suvir. *Eighteenth-Century British Literature and Postcolonial Studies.* Edinburgh University Press, 2009.

Keach, Benjamin. *The Banquetting House, or A Feast of Fat Things: A Divine Poem.* London, 1692.

Keach, Benjamin. *Spiritual Melody, Containing Near Three Hundred Sacred Hymns.* London, 1691.

Keach, Benjamin. *Spiritual Songs: Being the Marrow of the Scripture, in Songs of Praise to Almighty God, from the Old and New Testament.* London, 1700.

Keeble, N. H. *The Literary Culture of Nonconformity in Later Seventeenth-Century England.* University of Georgia Press, 1987.

Kidd, Thomas S. *The Great Awakening: The Roots of Evangelical Christianity in Colonial America.* Yale University Press, 2007.

Kidd, Thomas S. *The Protestant Interest: New England After Puritanism.* Yale University Press, 2004.

Kimbrough, S. T. "Charles Wesley as Biblical Interpreter." *Methodist History* 26 (1988): 139–53.

King, Giovan Venable. "Psalms in the Key of Life: Isaac Watts and the Composers of Negro Spirituals." *International Congregational Journal* 4 (2005): 41–58.

Kirk, J. Andrew. *What Is Mission? Theological Explorations*. Fortress Press, 2000.

Klauber, Martin I., and Scott M. Manetsch. *The Great Commission: Evangelicals and the History of World Missions*. B&H Academic, 2008.

Knapp, John. "Isaac Watts's Unfixed Hymn Genre." *Modern Philology* 109 (2012): 463–82.

LaGrand, James. *The Earliest Christian Mission to "All Nations" in the Light of Matthew's Gospel*. Eerdmans, 1999.

Lambert, Frank. *Inventing the "Great Awakening."* Princeton University Press, 1999.

Lamport, Mark A., et al. *Hymns and Hymnody: Historical and Theological Introductions, Vol. 2: From Catholic Europe to Protestant Europe*. Cascade, 2019.

Langmead, Ross. "What Is Missiology?" *Missiology: An International Review* 42 (2013): 67–79.

Latourette, Kenneth Scott. *A History of Christianity, Vol. 2: Reformation to the Present*. Prince, 1975.

Leaver, Robin A. "Isaac Watts's Hermeneutical Principles and the Decline of English Metrical Psalmody." *Churchman* 92 (1978): 56–60.

Louth, Andrew. "The Church's Mission: Patristic Presuppositions." *The Greek Orthodox Theological Review* 44 (1999): 649–56.

Macinnes, Allan I. *Union and Empire: The Making of the United Kingdom in 1707*. Cambridge University Press, 2007.

Mack, Phyllis. "Religious Dissenters in Enlightenment England." *History Workshop Journal* 49 (2000): 1–23.

Maclear, J. F. "Isaac Watts and the Idea of Public Religion." *Journal of the History of Ideas* 53 (1992): 25–45.

Maring, Norman H., and Winthrop S. Hudson. *A Baptist Manual of Polity and Practice*. 2nd rev. ed. Judson Press, 2012.

Marini, Stephen. "Hymnody as History: Early Evangelical Hymns and the Recovery of American Popular Religion." *Church History* 71 (2002): 273–306.

Marshall, Madeleine Forell, and Janet Todd. *English Congregational Hymns in the Eighteenth Century*. University Press of Kentucky, 1982.

Marshall, P. J. *The Making and Unmaking of Empires: Britain, India, and America, c.1750–1783*. Oxford University Press, 2005.

Martin, Linette. *Sacred Doorways: A Beginner's Guide to Icons*. Paraclete Press, 2002.

Martin, Roger H. "English Particular Baptists and Interdenominational Cooperation." *Foundations* 22 (1979): 233–45.

Martin, Roger H. *Evangelicals United: Ecumenical Stirrings in Pre-Victorian Britain, 1795–1830*. Scarecrow Press, 1983.

Martin-Achard, Robert. *A Light to the Nations: A Study of the Old Testament Conception of Israel's Mission to the Word*. Oliver & Boyd, 1962.

Massie, Allan. *The Royal Stuarts: A History of the Family that Shaped Britain*. St. Martin's, 2010.

Matthews, A. G. *Calamy Revised: Being a Revision of Edmund Calamy's Account of the Ministers and Others Rejected and Silenced, 1660–2*. Clarendon, 1934.

Mays, James Luther. *The Lord Reigns: A Theological Handbook to the Psalms*. Westminster John Knox, 1994.

McElwain, R. D. "Biblical Language in the Hymns of Charles Wesley." *Wesley and Methodist Studies* 1 (2009): 55–70.

Melbournensis. "St. Francis Xavier." *The Irish Monthly* 9, no. 97 (1881): 337–49.

Meyendorff, John. *Imperial Unity and Christian Divisions: The Church 450–680 A.D.* St Vladimir's Seminary Press, 1989.

Milner, Thomas. *The Life, Times, and Correspondence of the Rev. Isaac Watts*. Simpkin & Marshall, 1834.

Morris, J. W. *Memoirs of the Life and Writings of the Rev. Andrew Fuller*. Lincoln & Edmands, 1830.

Mouw, Richard J., and Mark A. Noll. *Wonderful Words of Life: Hymns in American Protestant History and Theology*. Eerdmans, 2004.

Neill, Stephen. *Colonialism and Christian Missions*. McGraw-Hill, 1966.

Neill, Stephen. *A History of Christian Missions*. Penguin, 1964.

Neuendorf, Kimberly A. *The Content Analysis Guidebook*. SAGE, 2017.

Nicholls, David. *God and Government in an "Age of Reason."* Routledge, 1995.

Nicolson, Adam. *God's Secretaries: The Making of the King James Bible.* HarperCollins, 2003.

Noll, Mark A. *A History of Christianity in the United States and Canada.* Eerdmans, 1992.

Noll, Mark A., David Komline, and Han-Luen Kantzer Komline. *Turning Points: Decisive Moments in the History of Christianity.* 4th ed. Baker Academic, 2022.

Norton, H. Wilbert. "The Student Foreign Missions Fellowship over Fifty-Five Years." *International Bulletin of Missionary Research* 17 (1993): 17–21.

Nuttall, Geoffrey F. "Methodism and the Older Dissent: Some Perspectives." *Journal of the United Reformed Church History Society* 2 (1981): 259–74.

Nuttall, Geoffrey F. "Northamptonshire and The Modern Question: A Turning-Point in Eighteenth-Century Dissent." *Journal of Theological Studies* 16 (1965): 101–23.

Nuttall, Geoffrey F. *Philip Doddridge, 1702–51: His Contribution to English Religion.* Independent Press, 1951.

O'Brien, Susan. "A Transatlantic Community of Saints: The Great Awakening and the First Evangelical Network, 1735–1755." *American Historical Review* 91 (1986): 811–32.

Olson, Roger E. *The Story of Christian Theology: Twenty Centuries of Tradition & Reform.* InterVarsity Press, 1999.

Orchard, Stephen. *Nonconformity in Derbyshire: A Study in Dissent, 1600–1800.* Wipf & Stock, 2009.

Orton, Job. *Memoirs of the Life, Character and Writings of the Late Reverend Philip Doddridge.* Salop, UK, 1766.

Pagden, Anthony. *European Encounters with the New World: From Renaissance to Romanticism.* Yale University Press, 1993.

Parker, M. Pauline. "The Hymn as a Literary Form." *Eighteenth-Century Studies* 8 (1975): 392–419.

Parris, David P. *Reading the Bible with Giants: How 2000 Years of Biblical Interpretation Can Shed New Light on Old Texts.* Paternoster, 2006.

Patrick, John. *A Century of Select Psalms, and Portions of the Psalms of David, Especially Those of Praise.* London, 1679.

Payne, Ernest A. "Eighteenth Century English Congregationalism as Exemplified in the Life and Work of Philip Doddridge." *Review & Expositor* 48 (1951): 286–301.

Payne, Ernest A. "Toleration and Establishment: A Historical Outline." In *From Uniformity to Unity, 1662–1962*, edited by Geoffrey F. Nuttall and Owen Chadwick, 255–88. SPCK, 1962.

Pearse, Meic. *The Age of Reason: From the Wars of Religion to the French Revolution, 1570–1789*. The Baker History of the Church, vol. 5. Baker, 2006.

Phillips, Christopher N. "Cotton Mather Brings Isaac Watts's Hymns to America; or, How to Perform a Hymn Without Singing It." *New England Quarterly* 85 (2012): 203–21.

Phillips, Christopher N. *The Hymnal: A Reading History*. Johns Hopkins University Press, 2018.

Phillips, C. S. *Hymnody Past and Present*. Macmillan, 1937.

Porter, Andrew. *Religion Versus Empire? British Protestant Missionaries and Overseas Expansion, 1700–1914*. Manchester University Press, 2004.

Porterfield, Amanda. *A People's History of Christianity, Vol. 6: Modern Christianity to 1900*. Fortress Press, 2010.

Rack, Henry D. "John Wesley and Overseas Missions: Principles and Practice." *Wesley and Methodist Studies* 5 (2013): 30–55.

Randall, Ian M. "A Missional Spirituality: Moravian Brethren and Eighteenth-Century English Evangelicalism." *Transformation* 23 (2006): 204–14.

Reynolds, William J., and Milburn Price. *A Survey of Christian Hymnody*, 4th ed. Hope Publishing, 1999.

Richey, Russell E. "Effects of Toleration on Eighteenth-Century Dissent." *Journal of Religious History* 8 (1975): 350–63.

Richey, Russell E. "English Baptists and Eighteenth-Century Dissent." *Foundations* 16 (1973): 347–54.

Rivers, Isabel, and David L. Wykes. *Dissenting Praise: Religious Dissent and the Hymn in England and Wales*. Oxford University Press, 2011.

Robert, Dana L. *Converting Colonialism: Visions and Realities in Mission History, 1706–1914*. Eerdmans, 2008.

Robinson, Robert. *A History of Baptism*. Lincoln & Edmands, 1817.

Roeber, A. G. "The Waters of Rebirth: The Eighteenth Century and Transoceanic Protestant Christianity." *Church History* 79 (2010): 40–76.

Rogal, Samuel J. *A General Introduction to Hymnody and Congregational Song*. Scarecrow, 1991.

Rogal, Samuel J. "Watts' *Divine and Moral Songs for Children* and the Rhetoric of Religious Instruction." *Historical Magazine of the Protestant Episcopal Church* 40 (1971): 95–100.

Romaine, William. *An Essay on Psalmody*. London, 1775.

Rorem, Paul. *Singing Church History: Introducing the Christian Story Through Hymn Texts*. Fortress Press, 2024.

Routley, Erik. *English Religious Dissent*. Cambridge University Press, 1960.

Routley, Erik. "The Eucharistic Hymns of Isaac Watts." *Worship* 48 (1974): 526–35.

Rutter, Robert S. "The New Birth: Evangelicalism in the Transatlantic Community During the Great Awakening, 1739–1745." PhD diss., University of Wisconsin, 1982.

Scherer, James A. "Missiology as a Discipline and What It Includes." *Missiology: An International Review* 15 (1987): 507–22.

Schreier, Margrit. *Qualitative Content Analysis in Practice*. SAGE, 2012.

Scottish Metrical Psalter: Psalms of David in Metre. 1650. Repr. Eremitical Press, 2007.

Secker, Thomas. *The Works of Thomas Secker, LL.D., Late Lord Archbishop of Canterbury*. London, 1825.

Seed, John. *Dissenting Histories: Religious Division and the Politics of Memory in Eighteenth-Century England*. Edinburgh University Press, 2008.

Sell, Alan P. F. "Approaches to Moral Philosophy Among the Eighteenth-Century Dissenters of England and Wales." *Jahrbuch für Recht und Ethik* 8 (2000): 263–313.

Shelley, Bruce L. *Church History in Plain Language*, 5th ed. Zondervan Academic, 2021.

Sherman, Robert. "The Catechetical Function of Reformed Hymnody." *Scottish Journal of Theology* 55, no. 1 (2002): 79–99.

Shiner, Rory. "On the Memorisation of Poetry in Childhood." *Quadrant* 65, no. 7 (2021): 108–10.

Simpson, Alan. *Puritanism in Old and New England*. University of Chicago Press, 1955.

Spinks, Bryan D. *Liturgy in the Age of Reason: Worship and Sacraments in England and Scotland, 1662–c.1800*. Ashgate, 2008.

Spurr, John. "Later Stuart Puritanism." In *The Cambridge Companion to Puritanism*, edited by John Coffey and Paul C. H. Lim, 89–107. Cambridge: Cambridge University Press, 2008.

Stanley, Brian. *The Bible and the Flag: Protestant Missions and British Imperialism in the Nineteenth and Twentieth Centuries*. Apollos, 1990.

Stanley, Brian. *Christian Missions and the Enlightenment*. Eerdmans, 2001.

Stanley, Brian. *The History of the Baptist Missionary Society, 1792–1992*. T&T Clark, 1992.

Steele, Anne. *Poems on Subjects Chiefly Devotional*. 2 vols. London, 1760.

Steinmetz, David C. *Reformers in the Wings*. Baker, 1971.

Stennett, Joseph. *Hymns Compos'd for the Celebration of the Holy Ordinance of Baptism*. London, 1712.

Stennett, Joseph. *Hymns in Commemoration of the Sufferings of Our Blessed Saviour Jesus Christ, Compos'd for the Celebration of His Holy Supper*. 1697. Repr. London, 1713.

Stephenson, William E. "Isaac Watts's Education for the Dissenting Ministry: A New Document." *Harvard Theological Review* 61 (1968): 263–81.

Sternhold, Thomas, and John Hopkins. *The Whole Book of Psalms, Collected into English Metre*. 1562. Repr. London, 1733.

Stevenson, Robert. "Dr. Watts' 'Flights of Fancy'" *Harvard Theological Review* 42 (1949): 235–53.

Stevenson, Robert. *Patterns of Protestant Church Music*. Duke University Press, 1953.

Stevenson, Robert. "Watts in America: Bicentenary Reflections on the Growth of Watts' Reputation in America." *Harvard Theological Review* 41 (1948): 205–11.

Stoughton, John. *Religion in England Under Queen Anne and the Georges*. Hodder & Stoughton, 1878.

Strivens, Robert. *Philip Doddridge and the Shaping of Evangelical Dissent*. Routledge, 2015.

Stroope, Michael W. *Transcending Mission: The Eclipse of a Modern Tradition*. Apollos, 2017.

Sykes, Norman. *Church and State in England in the XVIIIth Century*. Octagon Books, 1975.

Tapsell, Grant. *The Later Stuart Church, 1660–1714*. Manchester University Press, 2012.

Tate, Nahum, and Nicholas Brady. *A New Version of the Psalms of David, Fitted to the Tunes Used in Churches*. 1696. Repr. London, 1756.

Temperley, Nicholas. "'All Skillful Praises Sing': How Congregations Sang Songs in Early Modern England." *Renaissance Studies* 29 (2015): 531–53.

Templeton, Julian, and Keith Riglan. *Reforming Worship: English Reformed Principles and Practice*. Wipf & Stock, 2012.

Tenison, Thomas. *An Argument for Union*. London, 1683.

Terry, John Mark, Ebbie Smith, and Justice Anderson. *Missiology: An Introduction to the Foundations, History, and Strategies of World Missions*. Broadman & Holman, 1998.

Tilly, Charles. *Popular Contention in Great Britain, 1758–1834*. Routledge, 2005.

Tolmie, Murray. *The Triumph of the Saints: The Separate Churches of London, 1616–1649*. Cambridge University Press, 1977.

Townsend, James. "The Golden Age of Hymns: Did You Know?" *Christian History* 10, no. 3 (1991): 1–2.

Tucker, Ruth A. *From Jerusalem to Irian Jaya: A Biographical History of Christian Missions*. Zondervan Academic, 1983.

Turner, Daniel. *Divine Songs, Hymns, and Other Poems*. Reading, UK, 1747.

Van den Berg, J., and G. F. Nuttall. *Philip Doddridge (1702–1751) and the Netherlands*. E. J. Brill, 1987.

Wainwright, Geoffrey, and Karen B. Westerfield Tucker. *The Oxford History of Christian Worship*. Oxford University Press, 2006.

Walker, Williston. *A History of the Christian Church*. 3rd ed. Charles Scribner's Sons, 1970.

Wallace, Dewey D., Jr. *Shapers of English Calvinism, 1660–1714: Variety, Persistence, and Transformation*. Oxford University Press, 2011.

Wallin, Benjamin. *Evangelical Hymns and Songs*. London, 1750.

Walls, Andrew. *The Cross-Cultural Process in Christian History: Studies in the Transmission and Appropriation of Faith*. Orbis Books, 2002.

Ward, Kevin, and Brian Stanley. *The Church Mission Society and World Christianity, 1799–1999*. Eerdmans, 2000.

Water, Mark. *Parallel Classic Commentary on the New Testament*. AMG Publishers, 2004.

Watson, J. R. *The English Hymn: A Critical and Historical Study*. Clarendon, 1997.

Watts, Isaac. *Divine Songs Attempted in Easy Language for the Use of Children*. London, 1715.

Watts, Isaac. *Horae Lyricae: Poems, Chiefly of the Lyric Kind*. London, 1706.

Watts, Isaac. *Hymns and Spiritual Songs*. London, 1707.

Watts, Isaac. *Hymns and Spiritual Songs*. 2nd ed. London, 1709.

Watts, Isaac. *The Psalms of David Imitated in the Language of the New Testament, and Apply'd to the Christian State and Worship*. London, 1719.

Watts, Isaac. *Reliquiae Juveniles: Miscellaneous Thoughts in Prose and Verse, on Natural, Moral, and Divine Subjects*. London, 1734.

Watts, Isaac. *Sermons on Various Subjects*. 3 vols. London, 1721–1729.

Watts, Isaac. *The Works of the Late Reverend and Learned Isaac Watts, D.D.* 6 vols. London, 1753.

Watts, Michael R. *The Dissenters: From the Reformation to the French Revolution*. Clarendon, 1978.

Webb, Michael. "Heart, Spirit, and Understanding: Protestant Hymnody as an Agent of Transformation in Melanesia, 1840–1940." *Journal of Pacific History* 50 (2015): 275–303.

Wesley, John. "The Nature of Enthusiasm." In *John Wesley on Christian Practice: The Standard Sermons in Modern English*, edited by Kenneth Cain Kinghorn, 66–79. Vol. 3. Abingdon, 2003.

Whitley, W. T. *A History of British Baptists*. Charles Griffin & Co., 1923.

Wilkinson, John T. *1662—And After: Three Centuries of English Nonconformity*. Epworth Press, 1962.

Williams, J. B. *Memoirs of the Life, Character, and Writings of the Rev. Matthew Henry*. B. J. Holdsworth, 1828.

Wootton, Janet H. "The Wilderness and Christian Song." *International Congregational Journal* 10 (2011): 75–90.

Wright, Christopher J. H. *The Mission of God: Unlocking the Bible's Grand Narrative*. IVP Academic, 2018.

Wright, David F. "The Great Commission and the Ministry of the Word: Reflections Historical and Contemporary on Relations and Priorities." *Scottish Bulletin of Evangelical Theology* 25 (2007): 132–57.

Wykes, David. "From David's Psalms to Watts's Hymns: The Development of Hymnody Among Dissenters Following the Toleration Act." In *Continuity and Change in Christian Worship*, edited by R. N. Swanson, 227–39. Boydell, 1999.

Yates, Timothy. *The Expansion of Christianity*. InterVarsity Press, 2014.

Yeager, Jonathan M. *Early Evangelicalism: A Reader*. Oxford University Press, 2013.

More resources from

visit us at missionbooks.org

Missionary Motivations: Challenges from the Early Church

Matthew Burden

Beginning as an obscure sect in a backwater province of the Roman Empire, the Christian faith radiated out in all directions. What drove this expansion? Where some might think the missionary motivations would be the Great Commission or expressions of concern for non-Christians, which are common today, the early church's mission was profoundly Christocentric. The focus was exalting the reign of Christ and the pursuit of holiness. *Missionary Motivations* is the story of early Christianity's startling expansion. This book presents a deep look into the mindset that drove missional activity in the early church and explores original themes.

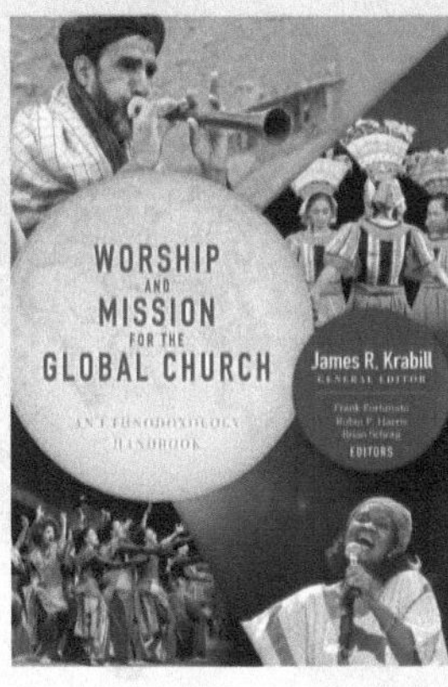

Worship and Mission for the Global Church: An Ethnodoxology Handbook

James R. Krabill, Frank Fortunato, Robin P. Harris, and Brian Schrag, editors

This book offers theological reflection, case studies, practical tools, and audiovisual resources to help the global church appreciate and generate culturally appropriate arts in worship and witness. Drawing on the expertise and experience of over one hundred writers from twenty countries, the volume integrates insights from the fields of ethnomusicology, biblical research, worship studies, missiology, and the arts.

Creating Local Arts Together–Revised and Updated: A Manual To Help Communities Reach Their Kingdom Goals

Brian Schrag

Creating Local Arts Together is a manual that offers a transformative approach to integrating local arts with kingdom work. The practical text reduces experience-based scholarly insights into a flexible seven-step process. In this revised edition, Brian Schrag has incorporated user feedback, lessons learned, and additional real-life stories of these principles over the last decade. This book includes an added index, periodic reflection questions, case studies from people applying CLAT in various contexts, updated references, and more content devoted to multicultural contexts.

www.ingramcontent.com/pod-product-compliance
Ingram Content Group UK Ltd.
Pitfield, Milton Keynes, MK11 3LW, UK
UKHW042020190726
13854UKWH00005B/2379